shape
shape2

First published in the United States in 2013 by Interweave Press

Interweave Press LLC
201 East Fourth Street
Loveland, CO 80537-5655 USA
interweave.com

ISBN: 978-1-59668-757-8
Cataloging-in-Publication data not available at time of printing.

Printed in China
10 9 8 7 6 5 4 3 2 1

JIBUNRASHIKU KIRARERU FUKUTACHI – HEIMEN KARA RITTAI NI KAWARU TOKI <II> by Natsuno Hiraiwa
Copyright © Natsuno Hiraiwa 2009
All rights reserved

Publisher: Sunao Onuma
Photography: Tadayuki Minamoto
Art direction and design: Eriko Kashiwagi
Styling: Natsuno Hiraiwa
Hair: TAKÉ (DADA CuBiC)
Make-up: Nao Suzuki (Eight pieces)
Models: Nanae Ubukata, Yuki
Sewing instruction and tracing: Shikano-room, Yumiko Sato
Pattern tracing: Kazuhiro Ueno
Production in cooperation with Taeko Sato, Kinu Naito
Editing: Haruyo Yamada

Originally published in Japanese language by EDUCATIONAL FOUNDATION BUNKA GAKUEN BUNKA PUBLISHING
BUREAU
English edition published by arrangement with EDUCATIONAL FOUNDATION BUNKA GAKUEN BUNKA PUBLISHING
BUREAU through The English Agency (Japan) Ltd.

English-language rights, translation, and production by World Book Media, LLC
Email: info@worldbookmedia.com

Translated by Atsuko Imanishi
English-language editor: Lindsay Fair

shape shape 2

Sewing for Minimalist Style

Natsuno Hiraiwa

INTERWEAVE
interweave.com

Contents

Introduction

Clothes are very personal. When you consider how much time we spend in our clothes and how much of our body they touch, it's no surprise that they possess the power to influence the state of our minds and our bodies.

Clothing becomes even more personal when you make it yourself. When you're involved in the construction process, you have the ability to customize the design to suit your size or style. You'll experience more excitement and satisfaction wearing a one-of-a-kind garment you made yourself than wearing anything you could have bought at the mall. As an added bonus, you'll discover the joy of sewing—an activity that can provide endless hours of relaxation.

When creating your own wardrobe, listen to your heart and don't worry about fashion trends. Choose fabrics you love based on color, pattern, and texture, not based on what's in style at the moment.

The designs in this book are versatile. Many of the garments can be worn multiple ways. In need of a more casual look? Simply fasten a few buttons to turn a skirt into a pair of pants. You choose how to wear a garment based on your style or mood.

I hope these designs inspire you to create clothing that is very special to you. If you find enjoyment in the creation process, I guarantee you will be happy with the results!

Double Circular Scarf

Instructions   46

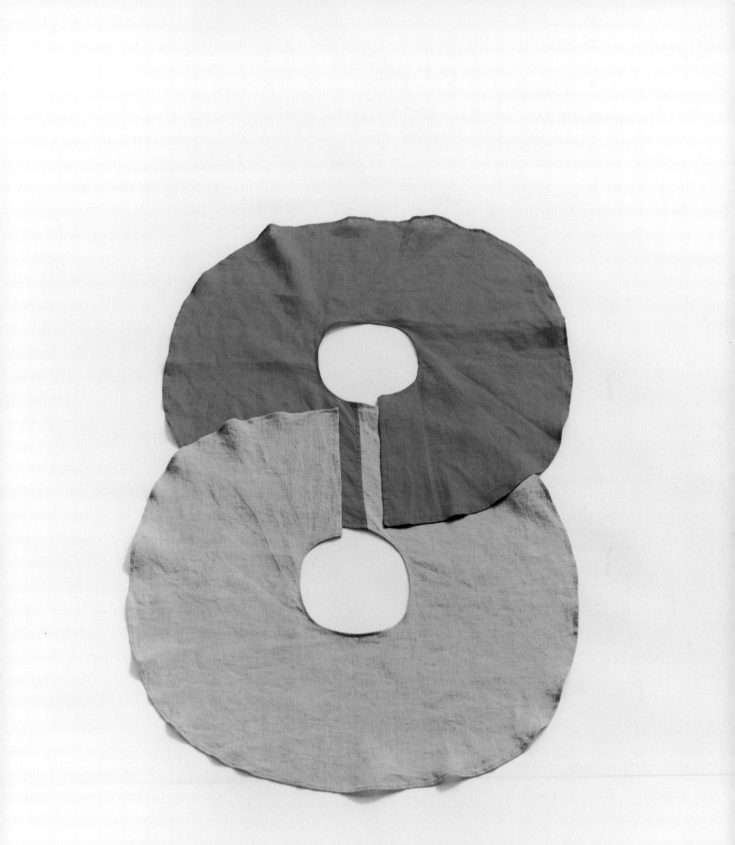

Double Circular Scarf,
made with two fabrics

Upside-Down
Bolero Jacket

Instructions   50

Layered Choker
Necklace

Instructions 57

Semi-Flared Gathered Skirt

Instructions 59

Reversible Belt with Hidden Pocket

Instructions 66

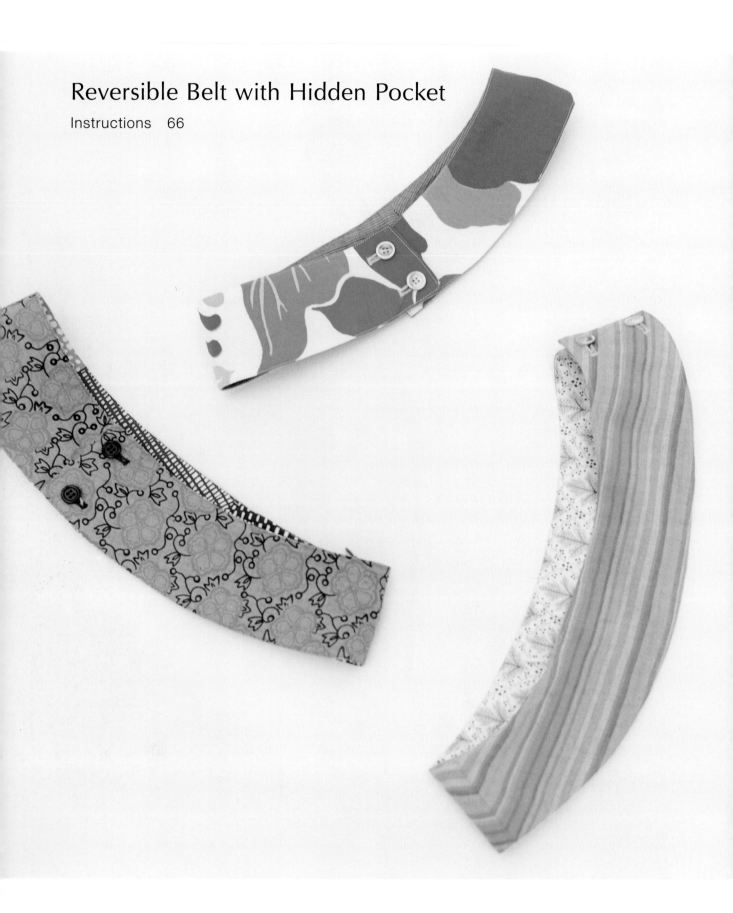

Double Layer Skirt

Instructions 71

Shown on opposite page:
a bird's-eye view of the
two layers of the Double
Layer Skirt.

Backless Vest/Stole
Instructions 77

Pleated French-Sleeve
Blouse shown without
a collar

Pleated French-Sleeve Blouse

Instructions   82

Pleated French-Sleeve
Blouse shown with
a collar

When making the Pleated French-Sleeve Blouse, consider
using the wrong side of a print fabric for a more muted look.

Puff-Sleeve Bolero Jacket

Instructions 90

A-Line Skirt/Harem Pants

Instructions 94

Buttoned-up: shown above as Harem Pants

A-Line Skirt/Harem Pants in brown, modeled on previous pages

Long Stole/Vest

Instructions   101

Long Stole/Vest, modeled on previous pages

Seamless Wrap Skirt

Instructions   106

Statement-Making
Spiral Brooch

Instructions   113

How to Make the Clothes

Before You Begin

FABRIC

Selecting your fabric is one of the most important steps when sewing clothes. Your fabric choice doesn't just affect the look of your completed garment, it also influences its comfort level and fit. For this reason, we've used natural fabrics, specifically cotton and linen, for the majority of designs in this book. We also recommend silk and wool, especially if you're interested in playing with texture or creating more season-specific garments. Have fun experimenting with different fabrics and let your instincts guide you. Here is some helpful information to keep in mind on your fabric selection journey:

Linen

Linen is perfect for summer because it absorbs moisture easily and releases body heat, which enhances the comfort of the wearer. Although linen is great for warm weather, it can be worn year-round when layered with heavier pieces, such as wool sweaters and tights. Linen should always be pre-washed as it shrinks slightly when washed. On the positive side, the more you wash linen, the softer it becomes. Always dry your linen in the shade in order to prevent discoloration. Linen doesn't stretch, but creases easily, so you may consider allowing for a bit more ease when sewing with linen.

Cotton

Cotton, the most popular fabric in the world, is often considered the most comfortable fabric. Much like linen, cotton absorbs and releases moisture in hot, humid weather and retains body heat in cold weather. In addition to being very strong and durable, cotton also has a soft hand. Organic cotton, which is grown without the use of artificial fertilizers, pesticides, or chemicals, is even softer than conventional cotton and is better for the environment. Cotton is easy to handle, so it's a great fabric to sew with, just remember to pre-wash it first as it often shrinks with the first wash.

Silk

Silk is a wonderful fabric to wear on warm days because it is lightweight and breathable. Known for its soft hand and fluid drape, silk creates airy, flowing garments. If you're a beginner sewist or haven't used your machine in a while, you may want to practice on a more forgiving fabric first as silk can be difficult to cut and sew.

Wool

Wool is best used for heavier garments designed to be worn in the autumn or winter due to its exceptional heat retention. Look for short-staple wool for warmer, more casual clothes and long-staple wool for more lightweight, formal clothes. There are many excellent wool blends available today that possess all the advantages of wool with added benefits such as durability and softness. Just make sure to check whether the fabric needs to by dry-cleaned as most wool shrinks and becomes matted when washed.

Pre-Washing Your Fabric

When working with linen and cotton, it's smart to pre-wash your fabric before cutting and sewing in order to prevent your finished garment from shrinking upon the first wash. To pre-wash your fabric, simply launder it as you intend to launder the finished garment. Depending on the fabric, this may mean machine washing and drying or hand-washing and line-drying.

Choosing Your Color Combinations

Many of the garments in this book are reversible. When selecting fabric for a reversible garment, make sure to consider color combinations carefully. Even though both colors will not be visible at the same time, it's best to avoid highly contrasting colors, such as black and white, as the darker color may transfer to the lighter colored fabric when laundered.

SIZING

The majority of the patterns in this book are in three sizes (small, medium, and large), while a few of the garments are one-size fits most. To determine your garment size, measure your bust, waist, and hips, then refer to the body measurement table included below:

	Small	Medium	Large
Bust	34" (86 cm)	37" (94 cm)	40.5" (103 cm)
Waist	28" (71 cm)	29" (73.5 cm)	32.5" (82.5 cm)
Hips	36.25" (92 cm)	39" (99 cm)	42.5" (108 cm)

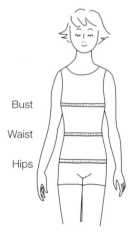

Bust

Waist

Hips

Keep in mind that any measurements noted in inches within the book are conversions of the metric measurements. Use the metric version of all measurements to ensure the most accurate fit.

The garments in this book are designed to fit the average height of 63" (160 cm). To determine whether you need to lengthen or shorten a pattern, measure the center back length, center front length, and/or inseam of the pattern and compare these measurements to your corresponding body measurements. It can also be helpful to measure the length of your favorite clothes as a reference to lengthening or shortening patterns. The best method for lengthening and shortening garments is called splicing, which involves proportionately altering pattern pieces without changing the garment's silhouette. It is important to select the correct splicing spot in order to ensure a well-fitting garment. The best location for splicing a shirt or dress is halfway between the bottom of the armhole and the bottom hem, while the best location for splicing a skirt or pants is halfway between the crotch and the bottom hem.

Once you've determined where you will make your splice, draw a perpendicular line and cut to divide the pattern into two separate pieces.

Patterns can be lengthened by inserting a strip of paper between the separated pieces or shortened by folding the pieces back to remove excess length. When splicing, remember to make the same adjustments to all matching pattern pieces, such as front and back.

GATHER YOUR TOOLS

Tracing paper: Use transparent paper to trace the pattern pieces from the pattern sheet.

Ruler: Use a ruler to mark seam allowances and measure out pieces without patterns, such as bias strips.

Highlighter: Use a brightly colored marker to distinguish the lines of the pattern pieces you need to trace. Using a highlighter to outline the pieces directly on the pattern sheet will make the lines easier to trace.

Pencil and eraser: Use a pencil to trace the pattern pieces onto tracing paper. Mechanical pencils draw clean, smooth

lines. Don't worry if you make a mistake or trace the wrong line—simply use the eraser to make it disappear.

Paperweights, tape, and pins: Use a paperweight or tape to hold the pattern in place when tracing the pattern pieces. There are special sewing paperweights available, but any heavy household object, such as a can, will work as well. Tape can also be used, just make sure it will not damage the pattern sheet upon removal. Use pins to hold the pattern in place when cutting out your fabric. Keep in mind that pins can leave marks on delicate fabrics, so you may want to use paperweights in certain instances.

Scissors: Use one pair for paper and one pair for fabric.

Tape measure: Use a tape measure to determine your size and to measure long or curved lines on patterns.

PATTERNS

Full-size patterns are included for most items in this book, with just a few exceptions. Once you've selected your size, follow these steps to prepare the patterns and cut out your fabric.

Trace the Pattern

1. Locate all the pattern pieces necessary for the garment. Use a highlighter to outline all the pieces directly on the pattern sheet. Make sure to outline all the marks included on the pattern pieces, such as the grain line, notches, and buttonholes.

2. Align tracing paper on top of the pattern sheet and secure it in place using paperweights or tape. Trace the pattern pieces using a pencil. When tracing corners, extend both lines a bit to preserve the exact angles. Draw short horizontal lines at the top of darts to mark them distinctly.

3. Copy the name onto each pattern piece and add important labels, such as fold line, center front/back, and openings.

Add Seam Allowances to the Pattern Pieces

1. Seam allowance is not included on the patterns, so it will need to be added. Refer to the cutting diagram included for each project to determine the seam allowances for each pattern piece. In this book, the seam allowance is ⅜" (1 cm), unless otherwise noted. Use a ruler to mark the seam allowances around each traced pattern piece. The seam allowances should be parallel to the pattern piece outlines.

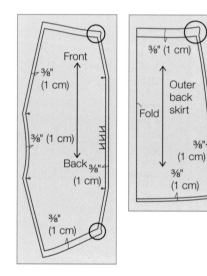

2. Cut out the traced pattern pieces along the seam allowances. Double-check that you have all the necessary pattern pieces.

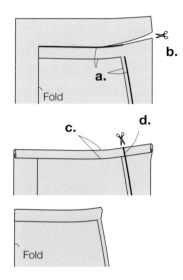

a. Mark the seam allowance lines parallel to the pattern piece outlines.

b. Cut out the traced pattern piece along the waist seam allowance.

c. Fold paper over twice at the outline of waist.

d. Cut out the rest of the pattern piece along the seam allowances.

Cut Out Your Fabric

1. Refer to the cutting diagram included for each project to arrange your fabric for cutting. If the fabric is to be folded, fold it with right sides together.

2. Pin the pattern pieces to the fabric as indicated by the cutting diagram, keeping the grain lines parallel to the selvage.

3. Cut out the pattern pieces.

4. Use a tracing wheel and colored tracing paper to transfer important marks from the pattern to the fabric. If your fabric is delicate, you may need to use chalk to transfer your marks instead. Now you're ready to sew!

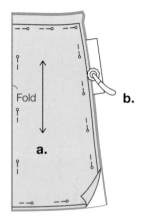

a. Cut out each pattern piece along the seam allowance lines.

b. Insert a piece of colored tracing paper between the fabric and pattern. Trace the seam lines and important marks with a tracing wheel.

Double Circular Scarf

Page 7 | Simply tie this scarf around your neck to show off the elegant drape created by the clever circular design. Use a single piece of linen, or combine two different fabrics to add contrast and texture.

Materials

Fabric A:
Thin linen 23¾" × 25½" (60 × 65 cm)

Fabric B:
Thin linen 23¾" × 25½" (60 × 65 cm)

✱ To make a solid-colored scarf, use one
25½" × 59" (65 × 150 cm) piece of thin linen.

Pattern (Side A)

Scarf

(Piece for this project is noted as *a* on pattern sheet.)

Cutting Notes

The cutting process must be very smooth for this pattern because of its curved shape. Use a rotary cutter to achieve a neater finish.

Sewing Tips

When finishing the edges, make clips along the seam allowance of the inner curve and cut notches along the seam allowance of the outer curve. This will make it easier to fold the seam allowances over and lead to a smoother curve.

Cutting Diagram

Fabrics A and B

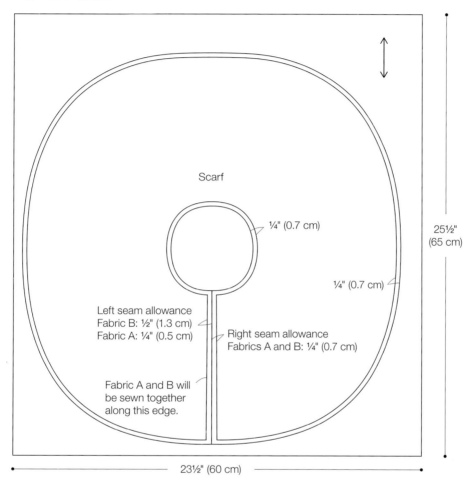

Scarf

¼" (0.7 cm)

¼" (0.7 cm)

Left seam allowance
Fabric B: ½" (1.3 cm)
Fabric A: ¼" (0.5 cm)

Right seam allowance
Fabrics A and B: ¼" (0.7 cm)

Fabric A and B will
be sewn together
along this edge.

25½"
(65 cm)

23½" (60 cm)

Construction Steps Overview

1 Sew Fabric A and B together.

2 Fold long edges over twice and stitch.

3 Fold short edges over twice and stitch.

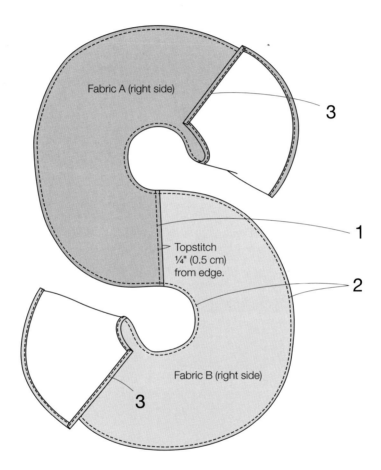

Fabric A (right side)

3

1

Topstitch
¼" (0.5 cm)
from edge.

2

Fabric B (right side)

3

1 Sew Fabric A and B together.

1a. Sew Fabric A and B together with a flat-felled seam to make S-shaped piece. When topstitching, use a ¼" (0.5 cm) seam allowance.

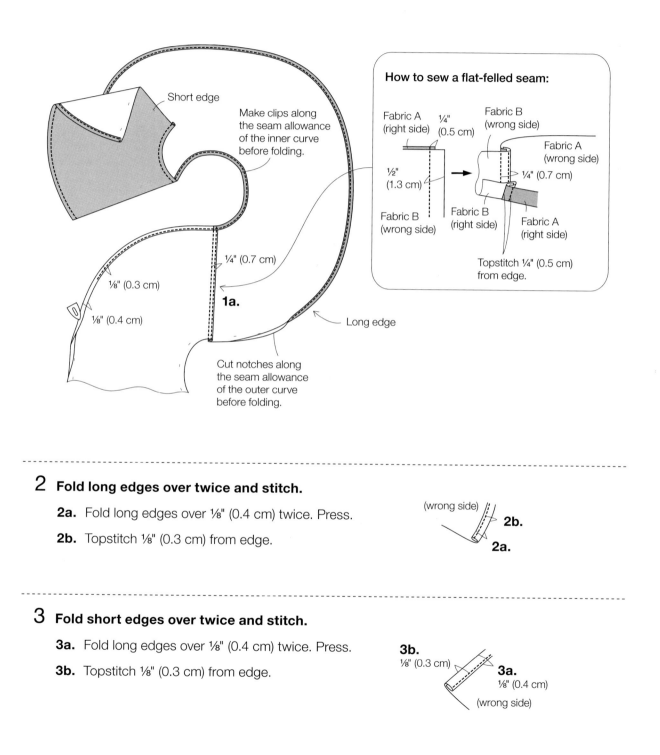

Short edge

Make clips along the seam allowance of the inner curve before folding.

How to sew a flat-felled seam:

Fabric A (right side) ¼" (0.5 cm) Fabric B (wrong side)

Fabric A (wrong side)

½" (1.3 cm) ¼" (0.7 cm)

Fabric B (wrong side) Fabric B (right side) Fabric A (right side)

Topstitch ¼" (0.5 cm) from edge.

⅛" (0.3 cm)

⅛" (0.4 cm)

¼" (0.7 cm)

1a.

Long edge

Cut notches along the seam allowance of the outer curve before folding.

2 Fold long edges over twice and stitch.

2a. Fold long edges over ⅛" (0.4 cm) twice. Press.

2b. Topstitch ⅛" (0.3 cm) from edge.

(wrong side) **2b.**

2a.

3 Fold short edges over twice and stitch.

3a. Fold long edges over ⅛" (0.4 cm) twice. Press.

3b. Topstitch ⅛" (0.3 cm) from edge.

3b.
⅛" (0.3 cm)

3a.
⅛" (0.4 cm)

(wrong side)

Upside-Down Bolero Jacket

Page 10 | This ingenious bolero is designed so it can be worn two ways: position the curved edge on top for a casual look or wear it with the angled edge on top for a more formal style. In just a few simple steps, you'll have two jackets in one!

Materials

Fabric: Cotton print or thin linen
44" × 67" (112 cm × 1.7 m)

Fusible bias tape (for angled opening edge): ⅜" × 35½" (1 × 90 cm)

Pattern (Side D)

Bodice

(Piece for this project is noted as *b* on pattern sheet.)

Cutting Notes

When cutting out the pattern, note that the seam allowance differs from the sleeve to the opening edge.

There are no pattern pieces for the bias strips. See cutting diagram on the following page for dimensions.

Sewing Tips

It is important to press each seam allowance before sewing in order to achieve neatly finished opening edges.

Consider fabric choice when finishing edges: If using thin fabric, fold the edges over twice and sew, as shown in the instructions. If your fabric is thin enough, you may be able to fold the sleeve cuffs over ¾" (2 cm) twice and sew, rather than finishing with bias strips. If using thick fabric, consider finishing all edges with bias strips to prevent bulky seam allowances.

Cutting Diagram

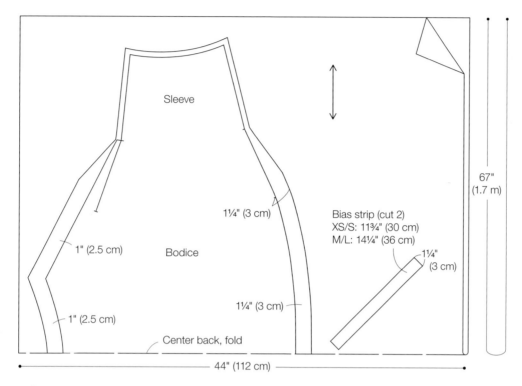

Sleeve

1¼" (3 cm)

1" (2.5 cm)

Bodice

1" (2.5 cm)

1¼" (3 cm)

Center back, fold

44" (112 cm)

Bias strip (cut 2)
XS/S: 11¾" (30 cm)
M/L: 14¼" (36 cm)

1¼"
(3 cm)

67"
(1.7 m)

✳ Seam allowance is ⅜" (1 cm), unless otherwise noted.

Construction Steps Overview

1 Fold the opening edges over twice and press.

2 Affix fusible bias tape to the angled opening edge. Fold over twice and stitch.

3 Sew the sleeves.

4 Fold the curved opening edge over twice and stitch.

5 Reinforce the end of the opening.

6 Finish the cuffs.

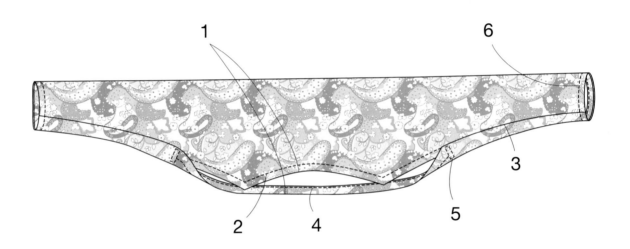

1 Fold the opening edges over twice and press.

1a. Zigzag stitch the sleeve seam allowances to the end of the opening.

1b. Fold sides over 1" (2.5 cm) and press. Tuck ⅜" (1 cm) under and press.

1c. Fold center over 1" (2.5 cm) and press. Tuck ⅜" (1 cm) under and press.

1d. Hand sew a running stitch along the seam allowance of the curved opening edge. Leave long thread tails.

1e. Pull the thread tails to gather the seam allowance into a curve. Press.

1f. Fold the cuffs over ⅜" (1 cm). Press.

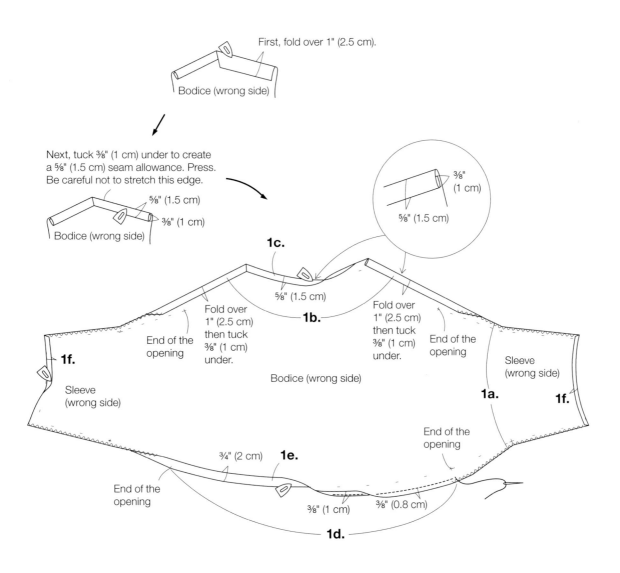

2 Affix fusible bias tape to the angled opening edge. Fold over twice and stitch.

2a. Affix fusible bias tape to the seam allowance of the angled opening edge by sewing in the middle of the tape.

2b. Fold over twice. Sew, starting and stopping at each end of the opening.

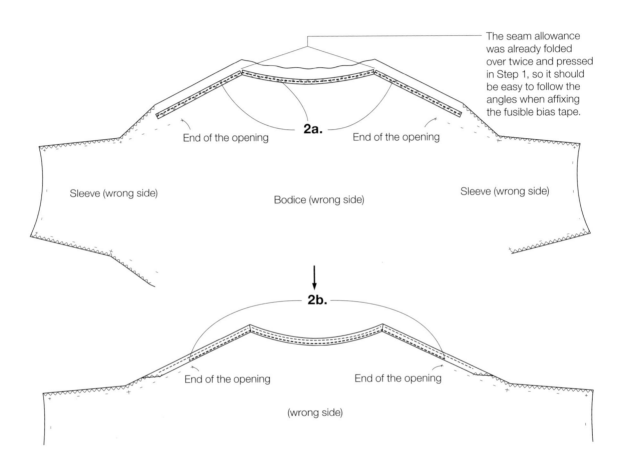

The seam allowance was already folded over twice and pressed in Step 1, so it should be easy to follow the angles when affixing the fusible bias tape.

End of the opening

2a.

End of the opening

Sleeve (wrong side)

Bodice (wrong side)

Sleeve (wrong side)

2b.

End of the opening

End of the opening

(wrong side)

3 Sew the sleeves.

3a. With right sides together, sew each sleeve, stopping at the end of the opening.

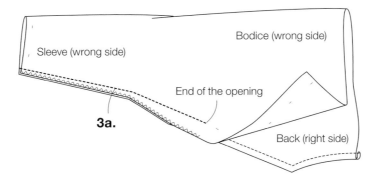

Sleeve (wrong side)

Bodice (wrong side)

End of the opening

3a.

Back (right side)

---

4 Fold the curved opening edge over twice and stitch.

4a. Press the sleeve seam allowances open.

4b. Fold the curved opening edge over 1¼" (3 cm) and press. Tuck ⅜" (1 cm) under and press. Stitch.

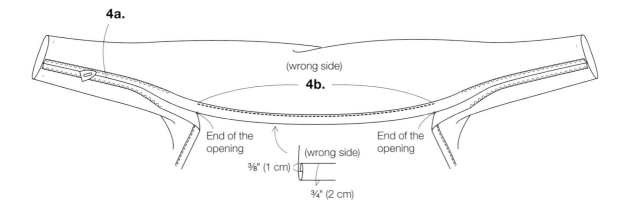

4a.

(wrong side)

4b.

End of the opening

(wrong side)

End of the opening

⅜" (1 cm)

¾" (2 cm)

5 Reinforce the end of the opening.

5a. Overlap the opening edge seam allowances and pin in place.

5b. Reinforcement stitch a ¼" × 1¼" (0.5 × 3 cm) rectangle on the right side. Repeat steps 5a.–5b. for other side.

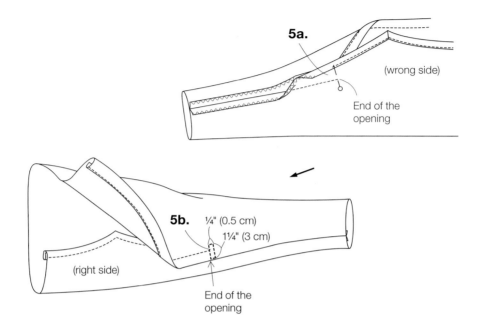

5a.

(wrong side)

End of the opening

5b. ¼" (0.5 cm)

1¼" (3 cm)

(right side)

End of the opening

6 Finish the cuffs.

6a. Make bias strip loops that are the same size as the cuff openings.

6b. With right sides together, sew each bias strip loop to a cuff.

6c. Turn the bias strips to the inside of the garment. Fold the bias strips over twice and stitch.

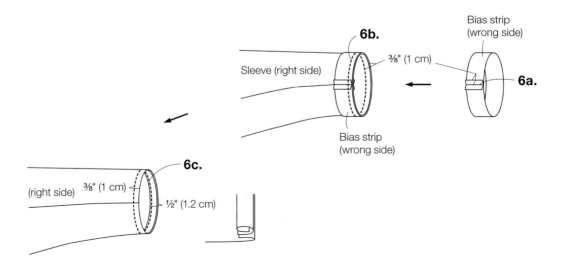

6b.

Bias strip (wrong side)

Sleeve (right side)

⅜" (1 cm)

6a.

Bias strip (wrong side)

6c.

(right side) ⅜" (1 cm)

½" (1.2 cm)

Layered Choker Necklace

Page 11 | Put fabric scraps to good use with this simple, yet elegant necklace. Wear it with one of the other designs to create a complementary look, or pair it with a basic t-shirt to make it stand out.

Materials

Fabric A: Printed fabric
6" × 6" (15 × 15 cm)

Fabric B: Striped fabric
4¾" × 9¾" (12 × 25 cm)

Crochet thread

Crochet hook: B/1 (2.25 mm)

Pattern (Side D)

Choker/Brooch

(Piece for this project is noted as I on pattern sheet.)

Cutting Notes

Cut out three pieces of Fabric A without seam allowance. Cut out six pieces of Fabric B without seam allowance and three pieces of Fabric B with a ¹⁄₁₆"–¼" (0.2–0.5 cm) seam allowance. It is not necessary to use the pattern pieces for this project—design your own necklace by layering any number of circular pieces of varying sizes. The raw edge of the fabric is part of the design of this necklace. To make the necklace appear less frayed, cut out pattern pieces on the bias.

Sewing Tips

If you don't know how to crochet, simply use a thicker thread as the chain for this necklace. Note that you will need less thread.

Cutting Diagram

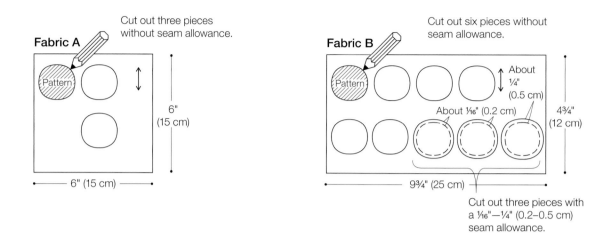

Fabric A

Cut out three pieces without seam allowance.

Pattern

6" (15 cm)

6" (15 cm)

Fabric B

Cut out six pieces without seam allowance.

Pattern

About ¼" (0.5 cm)

About 1⁄16" (0.2 cm)

4¾" (12 cm)

9¾" (25 cm)

Cut out three pieces with a 1⁄16"–¼" (0.2–0.5 cm) seam allowance.

Construction Steps Overview

1 Leave an 8" (20 cm) tail, then chain stitch until piece measures 7" (18 cm).

2 Stop chain stitching. Using a sewing needle, insert the thread through the Fabric A and B pieces.

3 Resume chain stitching for another 7" (18 cm), then leave an 8" (20 cm) tail.

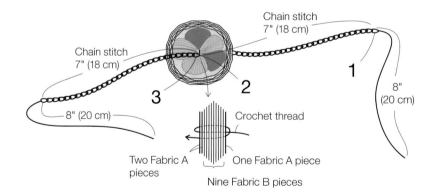

Chain stitch 7" (18 cm)

Chain stitch 7" (18 cm)

3

2

1

8" (20 cm)

8" (20 cm)

Crochet thread

Two Fabric A pieces

One Fabric A piece

Nine Fabric B pieces

Semi-Flared Gathered Skirt

Page 12 | Enjoy the benefits of both flared and gathered silhouettes with this double-duty skirt. Wear the darts in front for a classic look or turn it around and position the gathers and tie in front for a softer look. Since the flared section overlaps the gathers, this skirt is more figure-flattering than an ordinary gathered skirt.

Materials

Fabric A: Dark herringbone linen
43¼" × 43¼" (110 cm × 1.1 m)

Fabric B: Gray herringbone linen
39½" × 43¼" (1 m × 110 cm)

Pattern (Side A)

Back, Front, Back Facing, Front Facing

(Pieces for this project are noted as *c* on pattern sheet.)

Cutting Notes

There are no pattern pieces for the ties. See the diagram on the following page for cutting instructions.

Sewing Tips

When attaching the ties, be careful not to sew through the facing. When topstitching the facing, be careful not to sew through the ties.

Cutting Diagram

Fabric A

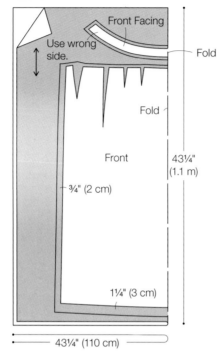

Front Facing

Use wrong side.

Fold

Fold

Front

¾" (2 cm)

43¼" (1.1 m)

1¼" (3 cm)

43¼" (110 cm)

✽ Seam allowance is ⅜" (1 cm), unless otherwise noted.

Fabric B

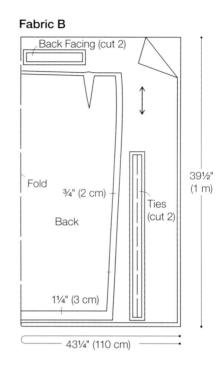

Back Facing (cut 2)

Fold

¾" (2 cm)

Back

Ties (cut 2)

1¼" (3 cm)

39½" (1 m)

43¼" (110 cm)

Tie Dimensions

Cut out the ties, which have no pattern, according to the dimensions in the diagram below.

Ties

Fold

⅝" (1.5 cm)

22½" (57 cm)

Facing Diagram

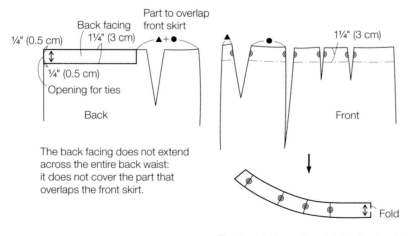

¼" (0.5 cm)

Back facing 1¼" (3 cm)

Part to overlap front skirt

▲ + ●

¼" (0.5 cm)

Opening for ties

Back

1¼" (3 cm)

▲   ●

Front

Fold

The back facing does not extend across the entire back waist: it does not cover the part that overlaps the front skirt.

The front facing will match the front waist once the darts have been sewn.

Construction Steps Overview

1 Sew the darts.

2 Finish the hems and sides of the front and back.

3 Make the ties.

4 Sew the front and back together.

5 Make the facing and attach it to the skirt.

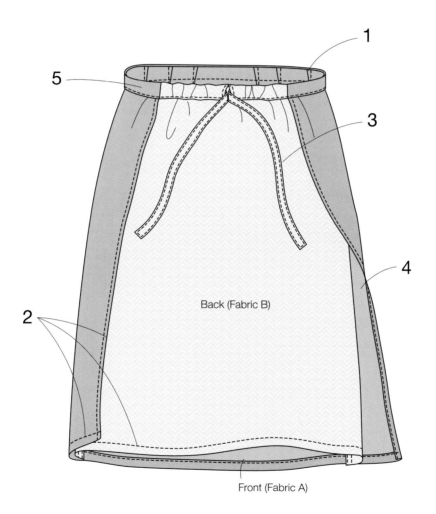

Back (Fabric B)

Front (Fabric A)

1 Sew the darts.

1a. Sew the darts on the skirt front. Press the seam allowances toward the center.

1b. Sew the darts on the skirt back. Press the seam allowances toward the center.

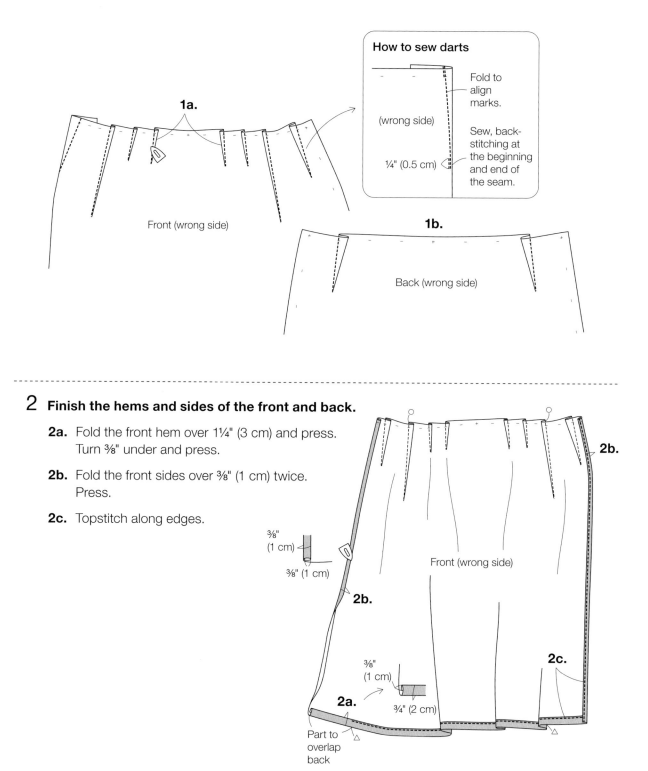

How to sew darts

(wrong side)

¼" (0.5 cm)

Fold to align marks.

Sew, back-stitching at the beginning and end of the seam.

1a.

Front (wrong side)

1b.

Back (wrong side)

---

2 Finish the hems and sides of the front and back.

2a. Fold the front hem over 1¼" (3 cm) and press. Turn ⅜" under and press.

2b. Fold the front sides over ⅜" (1 cm) twice. Press.

2c. Topstitch along edges.

⅜" (1 cm)

⅜" (1 cm)

2b.

2b.

Front (wrong side)

⅜" (1 cm)

2a.

¾" (2 cm)

2c.

Part to overlap back

2 Finish the hems and sides of the front and back (continued).

2d. Fold the back hem over 1¼" (3 cm) and press. Turn ⅜" (1 cm) under and press. Topstitch along edge.

2e. Fold the back sides over ⅜" (1 cm) twice to the right side. Press. Topstitch along edges.

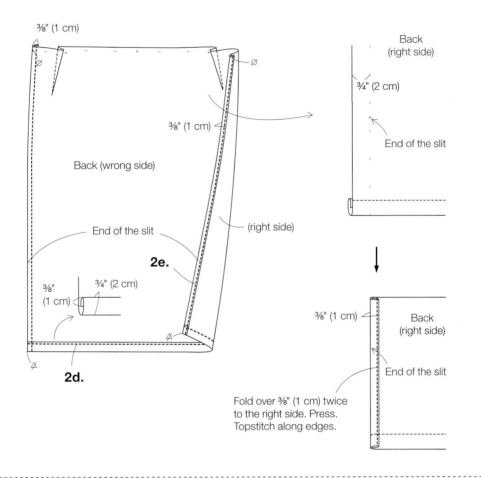

⅜" (1 cm)

Back (wrong side)

⅜" (1 cm)

End of the slit

(right side)

2e.

⅜" (1 cm)

¾" (2 cm)

2d.

Back (right side)

¾" (2 cm)

End of the slit

⅜" (1 cm)

Back (right side)

End of the slit

Fold over ⅜" (1 cm) twice to the right side. Press. Topstitch along edges.

3 Make the ties (make 2).

3a. Fold short edges in ⅜" (1 cm).

3b. Fold tie in fourths and topstitch.

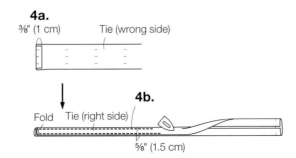

4a.

⅜" (1 cm)

Tie (wrong side)

Fold   Tie (right side)

4b.

⅝" (1.5 cm)

4 Sew the front and back together.

4a. Overlap front and back to align ○ and ⊘ marks. Baste across the top.

4b. Sew front and back together with two reinforcement stitch seams ⅜" (1 cm) apart. Stop at the end of the slit.

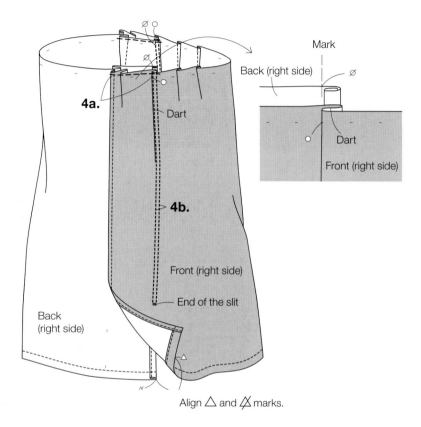

Align △ and ⚠ marks.

---

5 Make the facing and attach it to the skirt.

5a. With right sides together, sew back facings to each edge of front facing using a ⅜" (1 cm) seam allowance.

5b. Press seam allowances open.

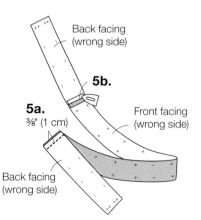

5 Make the facing and attach it to the skirt (continued).

5c. With right sides together, sew back facings together, leaving an opening for the ties.

5d. Topstitch around the opening using a ¼" (0.5 cm).

5e. Fold the edge of the facing over ⅜" (1 cm). Press.

5f. Sew facing to the wrong side of the skirt at the waist.

5g. Baste the ties in place using a ⅝" (1.5 cm) seam allowance.

5h. Fold the facing to the right side of the skirt.

5i. Pull the ties out through the opening in the facing.

5j. Topstitch the facing.

5k. Topstitch to secure the ties.

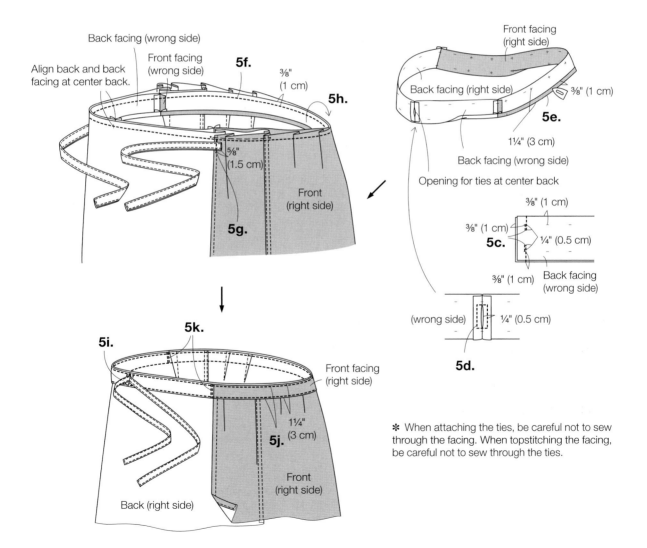

✷ When attaching the ties, be careful not to sew through the facing. When topstitching the facing, be careful not to sew through the ties.

Reversible Belt with Hidden Pocket

Page 14 | Transform your basic t-shirt and jeans into a fresh and unique outfit with this smart belt. With a hidden pocket perfect for storing necessities, this belt is the ideal accessory for shopping and traveling. Take advantage of the belt's reversible design by using fabrics with different colors and patterns to create one belt with two distinct styles.

Materials

Fabric A:
Striped cotton or linen
9¾" × 47¼" (25 × 120 cm)

Fabric B:
Printed cotton or linen
9¾" × 47¼" (25 × 120 cm)

Accent fabric (for pocket):
Cotton
6" × 11¾" (15 × 30 cm)

Lightweight fusible interfacing (for back):
23¾" × 35½" (60 × 90 cm)

Fusible bias tape (for back):
⅜" × 63" (1 cm × 1.6 m)

One 8¾" (22 cm) invisible zipper

Four ⅝" (1.5 cm) buttons

Pattern (Side D)

Back, Front, Pocket

(Pieces for this project are noted as *d* on pattern sheet.)

Cutting Notes

When cutting out the pattern, note that the back is not symmetrical. Feel free to make the back symmetrical if you prefer.

Sewing Tips

If using an 8¾" (22 cm) zipper, there may be a bit of extra length left over after installation. Sew the zipper in place and bar tack across the zipper at the desired length. To remove extra zipper length, cut 1" (2.5 cm) below the bar tack. Before cutting, make sure the zipper pull is above the bar tack.

Cutting Diagram

Main Fabric (A and B)

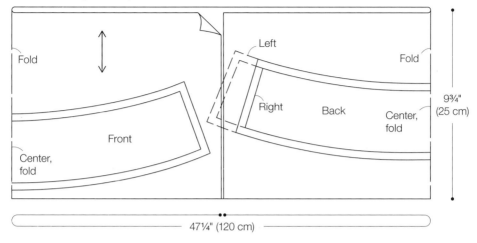

Fold

Left

Fold

Right

Back

Center, fold

Front

Center, fold

9¾" (25 cm)

47¼" (120 cm)

✳ Seam allowance is ⅜" (1 cm).

Accent Fabric (for pocket)

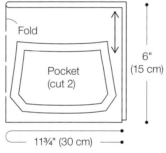

Fold

Pocket (cut 2)

6" (15 cm)

11¾" (30 cm)

Before You Begin Sewing

Fuse interfacing and affix fusible bias tape to the wrong side of the back.

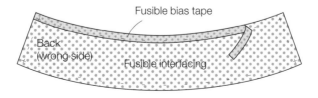

Fusible bias tape

Back (wrong side)

Fusible interfacing

Construction Steps Overview

1 With right sides together, sew front and back from Fabric A together. Press seam allowance open. Repeat with front and back from Fabric B.

2 With right sides together, sew Fabric A and B pieces together along the upper edge of the belt, leaving an opening for the zipper.

3 Install the zipper.

4 Attach the pocket to the zipper.

5 Sew the pocket together.

6 With right sides together, sew Fabric A and B pieces together along the remaining sides, leaving a 5¼" (13 cm) opening to turn right side out.

7 Turn the belt right side out and topstitch.

8 Make buttonholes and attach all four buttons (see pages 116–117).

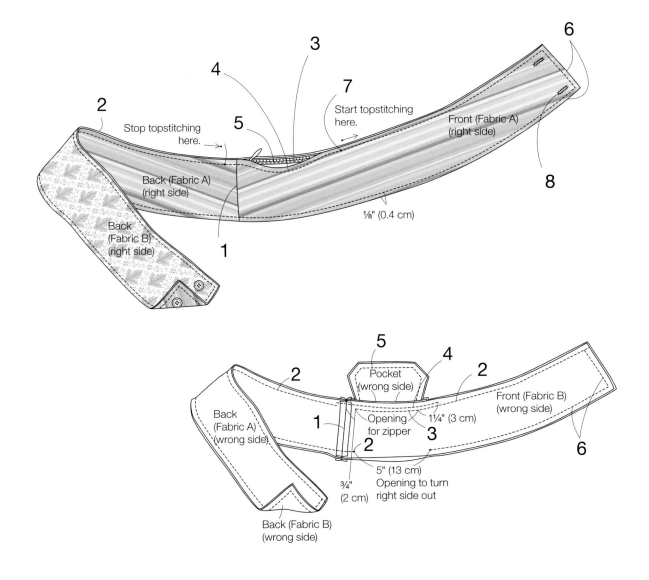

3

4

6

2

7

Stop topstitching here.

5

Start topstitching here.

Front (Fabric A) (right side)

Back (Fabric A) (right side)

8

Back (Fabric B) (right side)

⅛" (0.4 cm)

1

5

4

2

2

Pocket (wrong side)

Front (Fabric B) (wrong side)

Back (Fabric A) (wrong side)

1

Opening for zipper

1¼" (3 cm)

3

6

2

¾" (2 cm)

5" (13 cm) Opening to turn right side out

Back (Fabric B) (wrong side)

3 Install the zipper.

3a. Baste the zipper to the seam allowances of the front.

3b. Sew one side of the zipper to the seam allowance of the front from Fabric B along the upper edge of the belt.

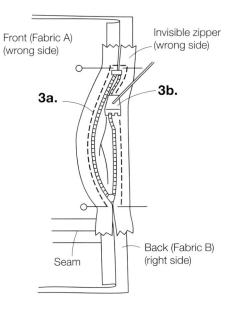

Front (Fabric A)
(wrong side)

Invisible zipper
(wrong side)

3a.

3b.

Seam

Back (Fabric B)
(right side)

4 Attach the pocket to the zipper.

4a. Sew one pocket piece to the attached side of the zipper using a ⅛" (0.4 cm) seam allowance.

4b. Sew the other pocket piece to the other side of the zipper, stitching through both the zipper and the seam allowance of the front from Fabric A.

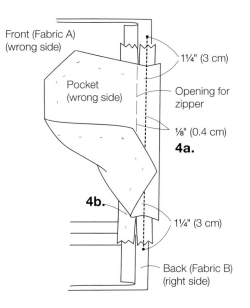

Front (Fabric A)
(wrong side)

1¼" (3 cm)

Pocket
(wrong side)

Opening for
zipper

⅛" (0.4 cm)

4a.

4b.

1¼" (3 cm)

Back (Fabric B)
(right side)

5 Sew the pocket together.

5a. With right sides together, sew the pocket pieces together, being careful not to catch the belt.

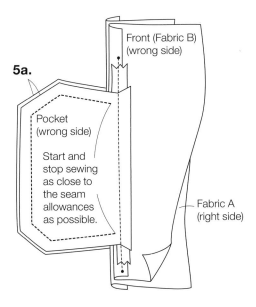

5a.

Front (Fabric B)
(wrong side)

Pocket
(wrong side)

Start and
stop sewing
as close to
the seam
allowances
as possible.

Fabric A
(right side)

7 Turn the belt right side out and topstitch.

7a. Turn the belt right side out through the opening. Fold and press the opening seam allowances, covering the bottom of the pocket.

7b. Starting on one side of the zipper and stopping on the other, topstitch around the entire scarf using a ⅛" (0.4 cm) seam allowance.

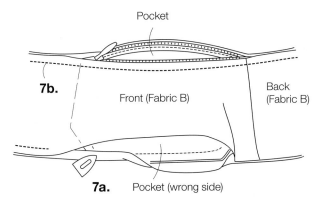

Pocket

7b.

Front (Fabric B)

Back
(Fabric B)

7a. Pocket (wrong side)

Double Layer Skirt

Page 16 | This double-duty skirt offers two different silhouettes: Align the layers at the side seams for a gathered skirt with a contrasting fabric band along the bottom hem, or twist the inner layer to create a voluminous balloon skirt.

Materials

Fabric A: Printed linen (for inner skirt)
55" × 59" (1.4 m × 150 cm)

Fabric B: Plain linen (for outer skirt)
33½" × 59" (85 × 150 cm)

Elastic tape (for waistbands):

(S): ¼" × 118½" (0.7 cm × 3 m), divided into four 29½" (75 cm) pieces
(M): ¼" × 128" (0.7 cm × 3.25 m), divided into four 32" (81.25 cm) pieces
(L): ¼" × 138" (0.7 cm × 3.5 m), divided into four 34½" (87.5 cm) pieces

Pattern (Side B)

Outer Back, Outer Front, Inner Back, Inner Front

(Pieces for this project are noted as *e* on pattern sheet.)

Cutting Notes

When selecting fabric, opt for lightweight linen. The heavier the fabric, the more voluminous the finished skirt. Due to this skirt's layered design, there is no need for a lining.

If using 45" (110 cm) wide fabric, determine the necessary length using the following formula:

skirt length × 2 (front and back) + seam allowance = fabric length

Sewing Tips

Make sure to zigzag stitch along the side seam allowances and hems of all the skirt pieces to prevent the fabric from fraying.

Cutting Diagram

Fabric A

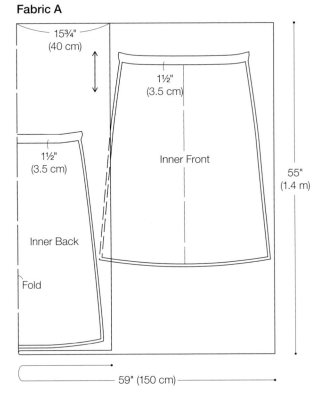

15¾"
(40 cm)

1½"
(3.5 cm)

Inner Front

1½"
(3.5 cm)

Inner Back

Fold

55"
(1.4 m)

59" (150 cm)

✳ Seam allowance is ⅜" (1 cm), unless otherwise noted.

Fabric B

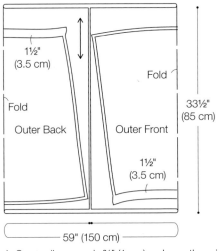

1½"
(3.5 cm)

Fold

Fold

Outer Back

Outer Front

1½"
(3.5 cm)

33½"
(85 cm)

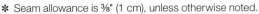

59" (150 cm)

✳ Seam allowance is ⅜" (1 cm), unless otherwise noted.

Construction Steps Overview

1 Sew the skirt pieces together along the hems.

2 Sew skirt front and back pieces together along the sides.

3 Make the waistbands.

4 Insert elastic tapes into the waistbands.

5 Fold the inner skirt to the wrong side and align the waistbands.

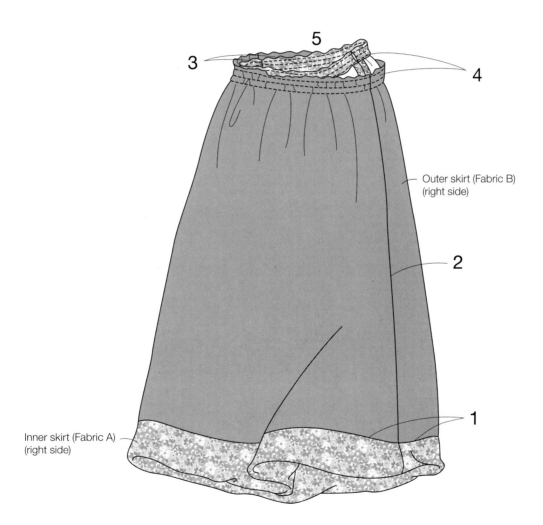

Outer skirt (Fabric B)
(right side)

Inner skirt (Fabric A)
(right side)

1 Sew the skirt pieces together along the hems.

1a. Zigzag stitch along the side seam allowances and hems of all skirt pieces.

1b. With right sides together, sew the inner front and outer front together along the hem. Repeat with the inner back and outer back.

1c. Press the seam allowances open.

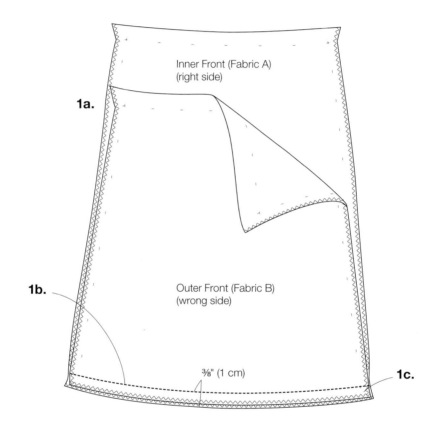

Inner Front (Fabric A) (right side)

1a.

Outer Front (Fabric B) (wrong side)

1b.

⅜" (1 cm)

1c.

2 Sew skirt front and back pieces together along the sides.

2a. With right sides together, sew skirt front piece to skirt back piece along the side seams. Make sure not to sew through the waist seam allowances on the left side.

2b. Press the seam allowances open.

3 Make the waistbands.

3a. Starting at the waist, sew Fabric A pieces together for ⅜" (1 cm), leaving the rest as an opening for the elastic tape. Repeat with Fabric B pieces.

3b. Topstitch the opening using a ¼" (0.5 cm) seam allowance.

3c. Fold the waist seam allowance of Fabric A over twice and stitch. Repeat with Fabric B.

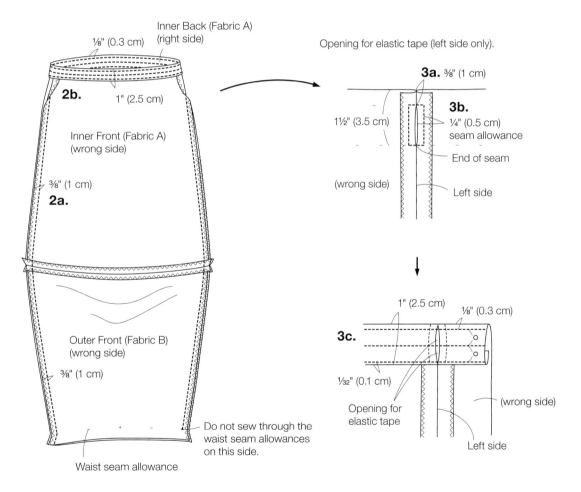

Inner Back (Fabric A) (right side)

⅛" (0.3 cm)

2b.

1" (2.5 cm)

Inner Front (Fabric A) (wrong side)

⅜" (1 cm)
2a.

Outer Front (Fabric B) (wrong side)

⅜" (1 cm)

Do not sew through the waist seam allowances on this side.

Waist seam allowance

Opening for elastic tape (left side only).

3a. ⅜" (1 cm)

1½" (3.5 cm)

3b.
¼" (0.5 cm) seam allowance

End of seam

(wrong side)

Left side

1" (2.5 cm)

⅛" (0.3 cm)

3c.

1/32" (0.1 cm)

Opening for elastic tape

(wrong side)

Left side

4 Insert elastic tapes into the waistbands.

4a. Thread two pieces of elastic tape through each waistband. Overlap the ends of each piece of elastic tape about ⅝"–¾" (1.5–2 cm) and sew together to secure. Hemstitch the openings closed.

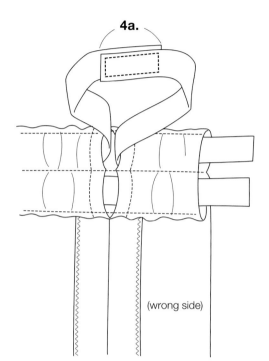

4a.

(wrong side)

Backless Vest/Stole

Page 20 | A truly versatile accessory, this piece can be worn three different ways. Fasten the buttons in the back to wear this garment as a vest, fasten the front button to wear it as a stole, or drape it around your neck to wear it as a uniquely shaped scarf. Since both sides of this garment are visible when you wear it, look for a double-sided fabric.

Materials

Main fabric: Lightweight wool
43¼" × 55" (110 cm × 1.4 m)

Lightweight fusible interfacing (for facing):
8" × 8" (20 × 20 cm)

Three ⅝" (1.5 cm) buttons

Pattern (Side A)

Bodice, Facing

(Pieces for this project are noted as *f* on pattern sheet.)

Cutting Notes

Note that both the right and wrong sides of the fabric will be visible on this garment since the collar is folded over. Make sure to choose a fabric that works on both the right and wrong sides.

Sewing Tips

Before sewing, use the pattern to check if the fold line sits in the right place on your neck. Positioning the fold line correctly will help achieve a more natural drape.

When finishing the back hem, you may need to make clips in the seam allowance to help fold the curved edges over smoothly.

Cutting Diagram

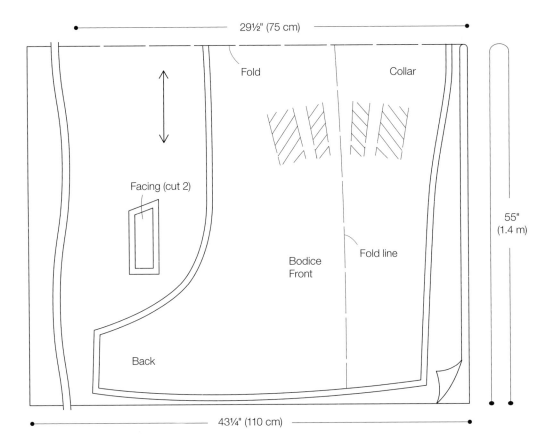

29½" (75 cm)

Fold

Collar

Facing (cut 2)

55" (1.4 m)

Bodice Front

Fold line

Back

43¼" (110 cm)

✽ Seam allowance is ⅜" (1 cm).

Construction Steps Overview

1 Finish the bottom and front hems.

2 Attach the facings.

3 Fold the garment into place.

4 Sew the tucks.

5 Make buttonholes and attach buttons on both front and back (see pages 116–117).

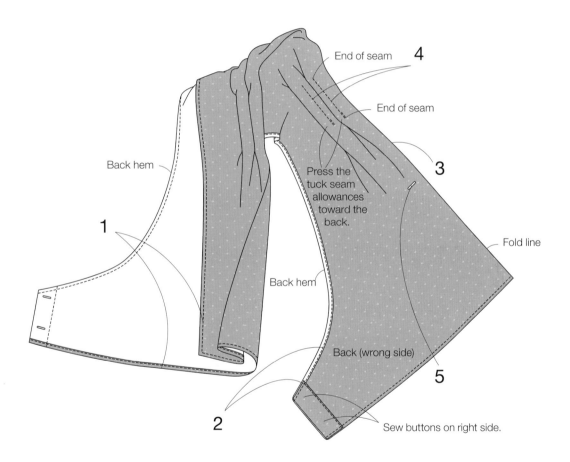

End of seam

4

End of seam

Back hem

Press the
tuck seam
allowances
toward the
back.

3

1

Fold line

Back hem

Back (wrong side)

2

5

Sew buttons on right side.

1 Finish the bottom and front hems.

1a. Miter the corners: Clip the corner seam allowances to ¼" (0.5 cm). With wrong sides together, fold the corners in half and sew using a ¼" (0.5 cm) seam allowance.

1b. Fold the bottom and front hems over to the right side ¼" (0.5 cm) twice and topstitch.

2 Attach the facings.

2a. Fuse interfacing to the wrong side of each facing piece.

2b. On each facing, fold the seam allowance over ⅜" (1 cm). Press.

2c. With right sides together, sew each facing to the back bodice along two edges.

2d. Trim seam allowances.

2e. Fold back hem over ¼" (0.5 cm) twice and sew.

2f. Fold each facing to the wrong side and sew along one side to secure in place.

2g. Reinforcement stitch the bottom edge of the facings along the bottom hem.

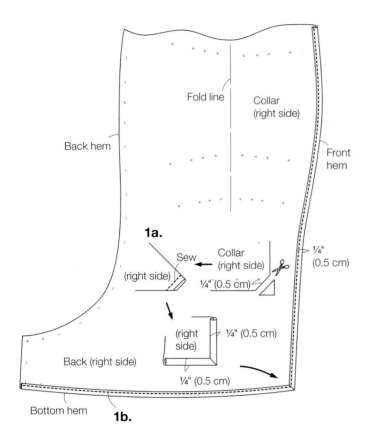

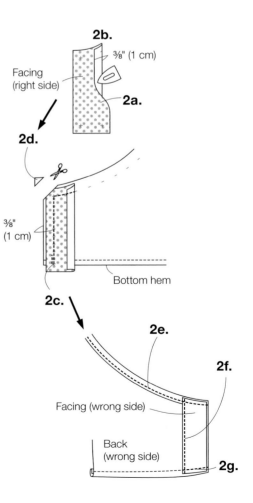

3 Fold the garment into place.

3a. Align the center of the bodice and the collar with right sides together.

3b. Fold the collar along the fold line.

3c. Fold to align the tucks on the wrong side and baste.

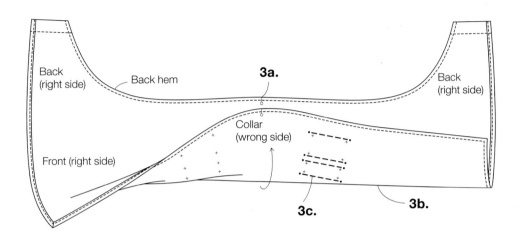

4 Sew the tucks.

4a. Sew the tucks in place, making sure to backstitch at the end of each seam. Press the seam allowances toward the back.

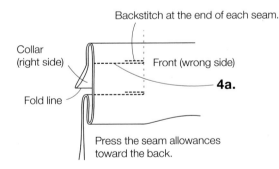

Pleated French-Sleeve Blouse

Page 22 | This easy-to-wear blouse combines a classic design with feminine details. Choose the variation that suits your style best: add the collar for a more formal look or forgo the collar and wear it unbuttoned for a more casual, minimalist look.

Materials

(for g-1 Pleated French-Sleeve Blouse with Collar)

Main fabric: Plain linen 55" × 59" (1.4 m × 150 cm)

Lightweight fusible interfacing (for back collar and facings): 25½" × 35½" (65 × 90 cm)

Five ⅝" (1.5 cm) buttons

Fusible tape (for center front edges): ⅜" × 43¼" (1 cm × 1.1 m)

Materials

(for g-2 Pleated French-Sleeve Blouse without Collar)

Main fabric: Striped cotton 55" × 59" (1.4 m × 150 cm)

Lightweight fusible interfacing (for facings): 15¾" × 29½" (40 × 75 cm)

Five ⅝" (1.5 cm) buttons

Fusible tape (for center front edges): ⅜" × 43¼" (1 cm × 1.1 m)

Fusible bias tape (for neckline): ⅜" × 23½" (1 × 60 cm)

Pattern (Side B)

Bodice (for g-1 and g-2), Collar (for g-1), Facing (for g-1), Front Facing (for g-2), Back Facing (for g-2)

(Pieces for this project are noted as *g* on pattern sheet.) The bodice pattern is divided into two pieces on the pattern sheet. Join at marks to complete the bodice pattern piece.

Cutting Notes

There are no pattern pieces for the bias strips. See cutting diagram below for dimensions. Cut out bodice first through two layers of fabric. Cut out remaining pieces from a single layer of fabric.

Sewing Tips

When folding the facings and bias strips to the wrong side after attaching them to bodice, take a slightly bigger fold so that the seam will not be visible on the right side of the garment. Press.

Finish the sleeves with bias strips cut from the main fabric, or if your fabric is lightweight, simply fold the edge over twice and sew.

Before You Begin Sewing

Affix bias tape to center front edges of g-1 and g-2 and to neckline of g-2.

Cutting Diagram

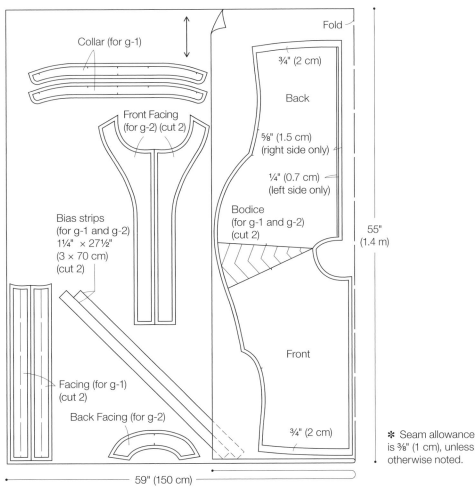

Collar (for g-1)

Front Facing (for g-2) (cut 2)

Bias strips (for g-1 and g-2)
1¼" × 27½"
(3 × 70 cm)
(cut 2)

Facing (for g-1) (cut 2)

Back Facing (for g-2)

Fold

¾" (2 cm)

Back

⅝" (1.5 cm) (right side only)

¼" (0.7 cm) (left side only)

Bodice (for g-1 and g-2) (cut 2)

Front

¾" (2 cm)

55" (1.4 m)

✳ Seam allowance is ⅜" (1 cm), unless otherwise noted.

59" (150 cm)

Construction Steps Overview

Variations g-1 and g-2

1 Sew the bodice together at center back using a flat-felled seam (see page 49).

2 Sew the bodice together at sides.

3 Finish the sleeve edges.

4 Make the shoulder pleats.

Variation g-2

5 Attach the facings.

6 Finish the facing and bottom hem.

7 Make buttonholes and attach the buttons (see pages 116–117).

Variation g-1

5 Attach the facings.

6 Finish the facing and bottom hem.

7 Attach the collar.

8 Make buttonholes and attach the buttons (see pages 116–117).

Variation g-2

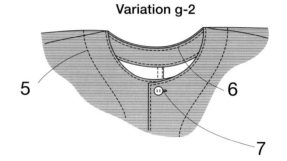

Variation g-1

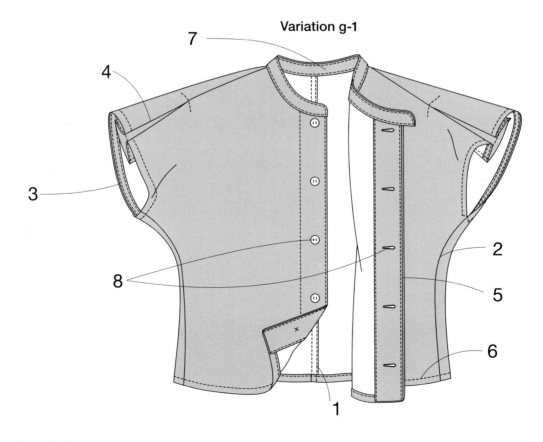

2 Variations g-1 and g-2: Sew the bodice together at sides.

2a. With right sides together, sew the bodice together at sides, stopping at the sleeve seam allowances of ⅜" (1 cm).

2b. Zigzag stitch each side seam allowance.

2c. Press seam allowances open.

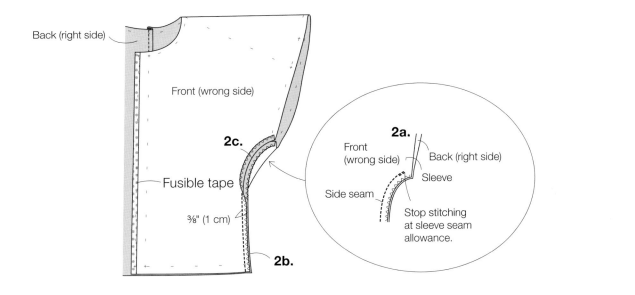

3 Variations g-1 and g-2: Finish the sleeve edges.

3a. With right sides together, sew a bias strip to each sleeve using a ⅜" (1 cm) seam allowance.

3b. Topstitch each bias strip on the right side, stitching close to the seam allowance.

3c. Fold the bias strip to the wrong side. Topstitch on the right side using a ⅜" (1 cm) seam allowance.

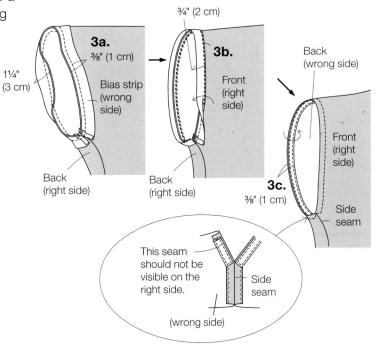

4 Variations g-1 and g-2: Make the shoulder pleats.

4a. Sew along the shoulder line to the end of seam marker. Fold the box pleats.

4b. Stitching through the two pleat layers only, sew each pleat together for as far as possible on each side of the pleat.

4c. On the right side, reinforcement stitch across the pleat to secure it in place.

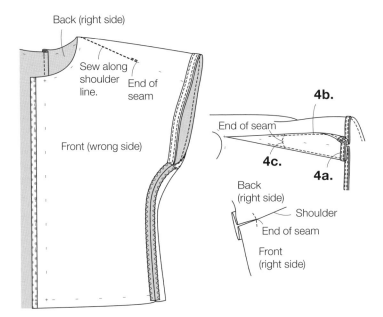

5 Variation g-1: Attach the facings.

5a. Fuse interfacing to the wrong side of the facings. Fold one edge of each facing over ⅜" (1 cm) and press.

5b. With right sides together, sew each facing to the bodice at center front using a ⅜" (1 cm) seam allowance. Trim seam allowances.

5c. Turn facing to the wrong side.

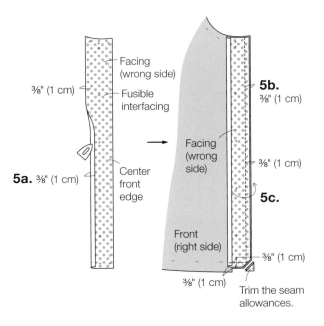

5 Variation g-2: Attach the facings.

5a. Fuse interfacing to the wrong side of the front and back facings.

5b. With right sides together, sew front facings to the back facing at the shoulders. Press seam allowances open.

5c. Fold ⅜" (1 cm) from the edge. Press.

5d. With right sides together, sew the facing to the bodice using a ⅜" (1 cm) seam allowance.

5e. Trim the seam allowances.

5f. Make clips in the curved section of the seam allowance.

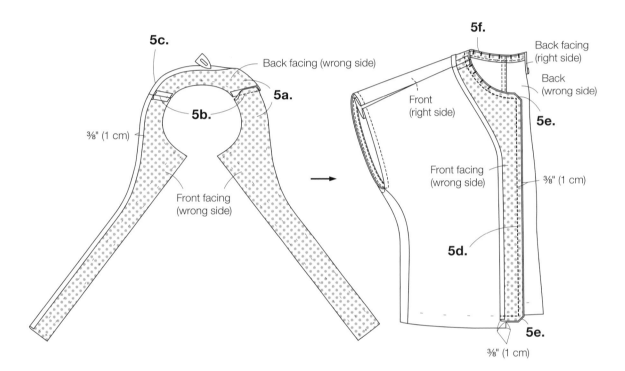

6 Variation g-1: Finish the facing and bottom hem.

6a. Topstitch the facing using ¹⁄₃₂" (0.1 cm) seam allowances to secure in place.

6b. Fold the bottom hem over twice and sew using a ³⁄₈" (1 cm) seam allowance.

6 Variation g-2: Finish the facing and bottom hem.

6a. Topstitch the facing using ¹⁄₃₂" (0.1 cm) seam allowances to secure in place.

6b. Fold the bottom hem over twice and sew using a ³⁄₈" (1 cm) seam allowance.

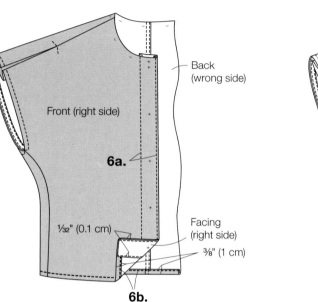

Back (wrong side)

Front (right side)

6a.

¹⁄₃₂" (0.1 cm)

Facing (right side)

³⁄₈" (1 cm)

6b.

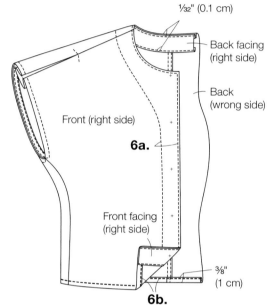

¹⁄₃₂" (0.1 cm)

Back facing (right side)

Back (wrong side)

Front (right side)

6a.

Front facing (right side)

³⁄₈" (1 cm)

6b.

7 Variation g-1: Attach the collar.

7a. Fuse interfacing to the wrong side of the back collar.

7b. With right sides together, sew front and back collar along three edges, starting and stopping at the seam allowances.

7c. Fold the front collar seam allowance and press.

7d. Turn the collar right side out.

7e. Sew the right side of the back collar to the wrong side of the bodice.

7f. Tuck the seams allowances under the collar.

7g. Topstitch the collar on the right side using ⅟₃₂" (0.1 cm) seam allowances.

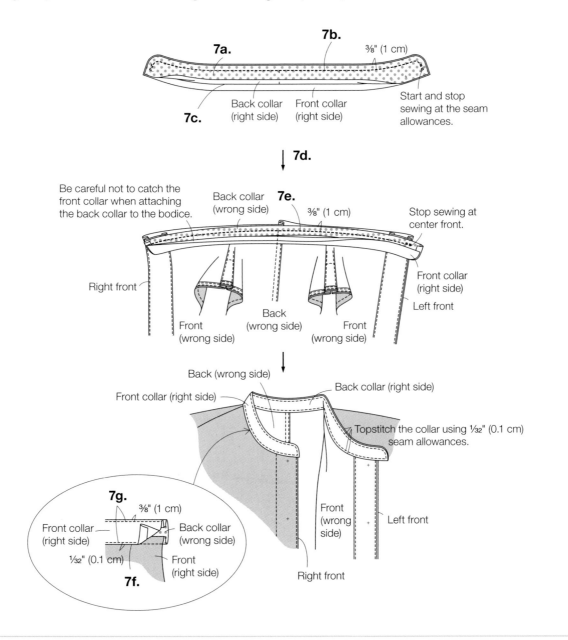

Puff-Sleeve Bolero Jacket

Page 26 │ This easy-to-wear bolero is also easy-to-make. With just a few seams and little tucks at the sleeves to add some volume, this jacket stitches up in no time. Use colorful print fabric for a bit of fun or opt for neutrals for a piece that goes with everything.

Materials

Main fabric: Printed cotton 17¾" × 118½" (45 cm × 3 m) or three tenugui towels

Lightweight fusible interfacing (for facing): 9¾" × 27½" (25 × 70 cm)

Fusible bias tape (for neckline): ⅜" × 51¼" (1 cm × 1.3 m)

Pattern (Side C)

Bodice, Facing

(Pieces for this project are noted as *h* on pattern sheet.)

Cutting Notes

This garment was originally designed to be made from tenugui towels, which are traditional Japanese hand towels made of thin cotton. Authentic tenugui towels are readily available online, but regular fabric will work as well. Since tenugui towels are narrow, the pattern is positioned on the edge of the fabric. If using regular fabric, position the pattern in the middle of the fabric and cut it out as usual.

Sewing Tips

Make sure to affix the fusible bias tape and zigzag stitch the seam allowances as shown in order to prevent the seams from fraying.

Cutting Diagram

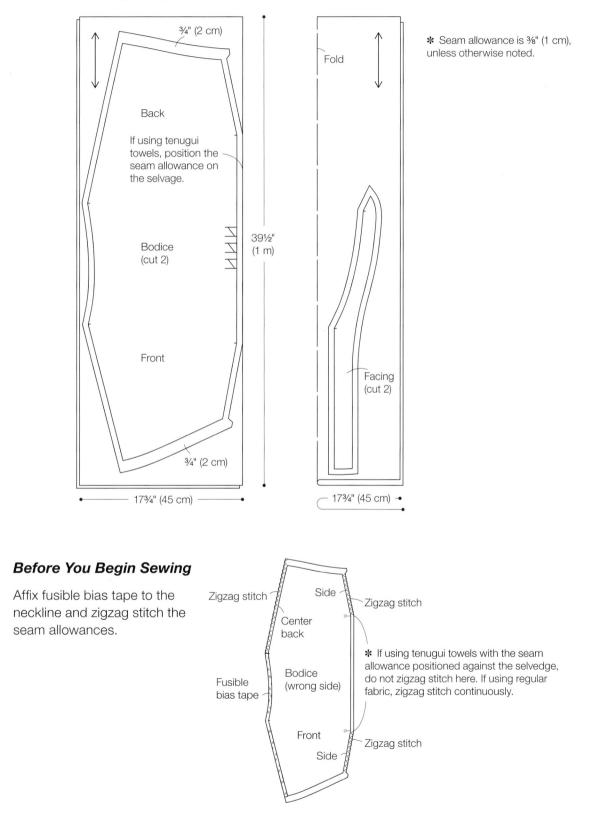

¾" (2 cm)

Back

If using tenugui towels, position the seam allowance on the selvage.

Bodice (cut 2)

Front

¾" (2 cm)

17¾" (45 cm)

39½" (1 m)

Fold

Facing (cut 2)

17¾" (45 cm)

✻ Seam allowance is ⅜" (1 cm), unless otherwise noted.

Before You Begin Sewing

Affix fusible bias tape to the neckline and zigzag stitch the seam allowances.

Zigzag stitch

Side

Zigzag stitch

Center back

Fusible bias tape

Bodice (wrong side)

Front

Side

Zigzag stitch

Zigzag stitch

✻ If using tenugui towels with the seam allowance positioned against the selvedge, do not zigzag stitch here. If using regular fabric, zigzag stitch continuously.

Construction Steps Overview

1 Sew bodices together at center back, stopping at the marker. Press seam allowance open.

2 Attach the facing.

3 Make the tucks.

4 With right sides together, sew the bodice together at the sides. Press seam allowances open.

5 Fold ⅜" (1 cm) over twice and topstitch to finish the sleeves.

6 Fold the hem over ⅜" (1 cm) twice and sew.

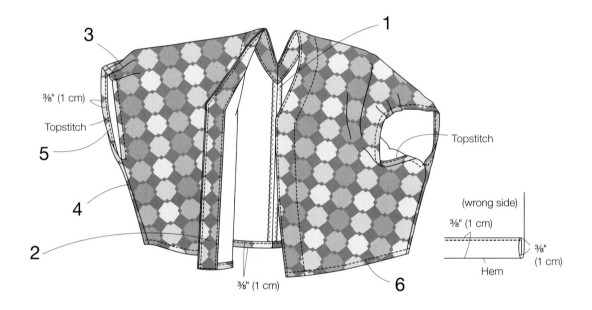

2 Attach the facing.

2a. Fuse interfacing to the wrong side of each facing.

2b. Sew facings together at center back, stopping at the seam allowance.

2c. Fold ⅜" (1 cm) over and press.

2d. With right sides together, sew the facing to the bodice. Trim seam allowances.

2e. Turn the facing to the wrong side.

2f. Fold the bottom hem over ⅜" (1 cm) twice. Press.

2g. Baste the facing in place. Topstitch using ¹⁄₁₆" (0.2 cm) seam allowances.

3 Make the tucks.

3a. Fold the tucks and baste to secure in place.

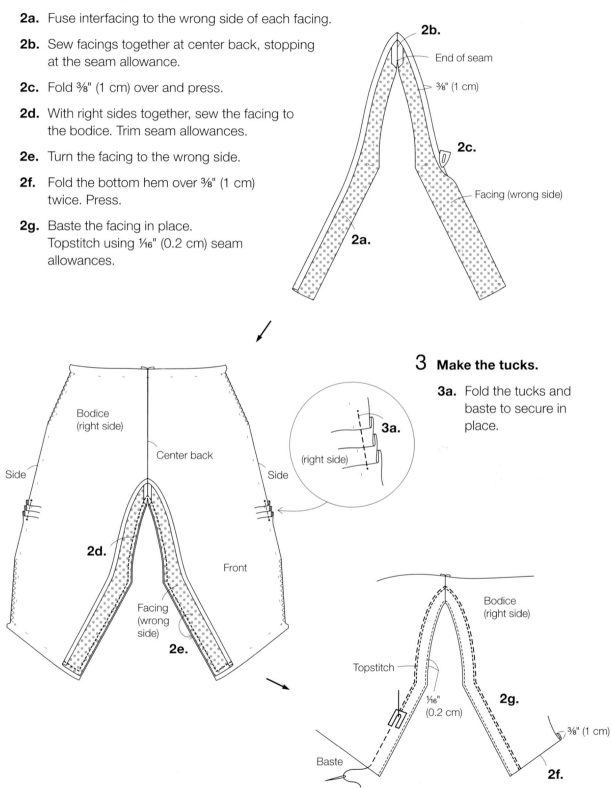

A-Line Skirt/Harem Pants

Page 28 | A few cleverly placed buttons allow this garment to be worn three ways! Fasten the buttons to create a pair of fashion-forward harem pants, leave the garment unbuttoned for a simple A-line skirt, or fasten the buttons on the outside for a skirt with a more tapered silhouette.

Materials

Main fabric:
Plain linen 59" × 71" (150 cm × 1.8 m)

Lightweight fusible interfacing
(for hem facings): 14" × 14" (35 × 35 cm)

Elastic tape: ⅜" × 55" (0.9 cm × 1.4 m)

Four ⅝" (1.5 cm) buttons

Pattern (Side C)

Back, Side Back, Back Waist Facing, Back Hem Facing, Front, Side Front, Front Waist Facing, Front Hem Facing

(Pieces for this project are noted as *i* on pattern sheet.)

Cutting Notes

When cutting out the pattern, first cut out a 1½" × 65" (4 × 165 cm) tie from a single layer of fabric. Then fold the fabric in half and cut out the other pieces.

Sewing Tips

Make clips in the seam allowance of the waist facing and hem facings before folding over to achieve a neater finish.

Cutting Diagram

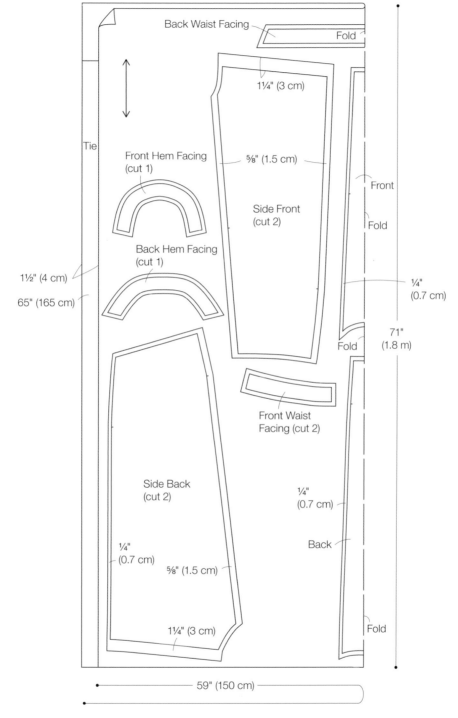

Back Waist Facing

Fold

1¼" (3 cm)

⅝" (1.5 cm)

Tie

Front Hem Facing
(cut 1)

Side Front
(cut 2)

Front

Fold

Back Hem Facing
(cut 1)

1½" (4 cm)

65" (165 cm)

¼"
(0.7 cm)

71"
(1.8 m)

Fold

Front Waist
Facing (cut 2)

Side Back
(cut 2)

¼"
(0.7 cm)

¼"
(0.7 cm)

⅝" (1.5 cm)

Back

1¼" (3 cm)

Fold

59" (150 cm)

✳ Seam allowance is ⅜" (1 cm), unless otherwise noted.

Construction Steps Overview

1 Sew the skirt together.

2 Attach the hem facings.

3 Finish the hem.

4 Finish the waistband.

5 Insert the tie.

6 Make buttonholes and attach the buttons (see pages 116–117).

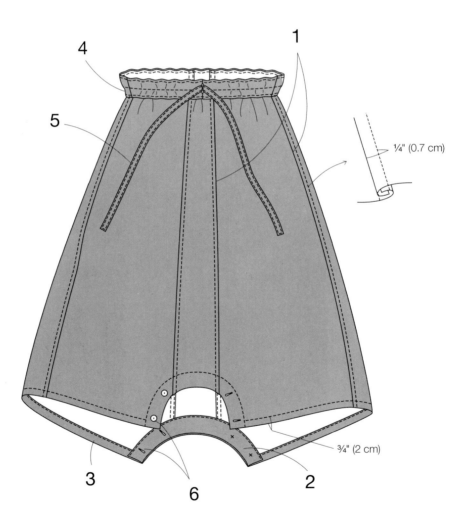

1 Sew the skirt together.

1a. Sew the front, side front, side back, and back pieces together with flat-felled seams (see page 49).

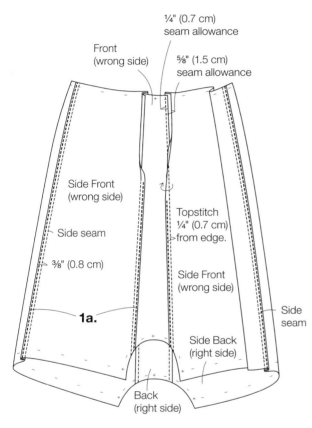

¼" (0.7 cm) seam allowance

Front (wrong side)

⅝" (1.5 cm) seam allowance

Side Front (wrong side)

Side seam

⅜" (0.8 cm)

1a.

Topstitch ¼" (0.7 cm) from edge.

Side Front (wrong side)

Side seam

Side Back (right side)

Back (right side)

2 Attach the hem facings.

2a. Fuse interfacing to the wrong side of the front and back hem facings.

2b. Fold over ⅜" (1 cm) and press.

2c. With right sides together, sew hem facings to the skirt using a ⅜" (1 cm) seam allowance.

2d. Trim the seam allowances.

2e. Make clips in the curved sections of the seam allowances.

2f. Fold the facings to the wrong side. Fold the bottom hem of the skirt over ¾" (2 cm) twice. Press.

2g. Topstitch the facings to secure in place.

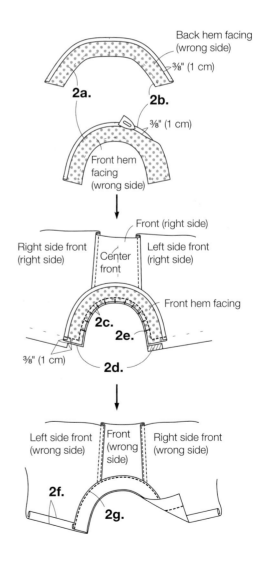

Back hem facing (wrong side)

⅜" (1 cm)

2a.

2b.

⅜" (1 cm)

Front hem facing (wrong side)

Front (right side)

Right side front (right side)

Center front

Left side front (right side)

Front hem facing

2c.

2e.

⅜" (1 cm)

2d.

Left side front (wrong side)

Front (wrong side)

Right side front (wrong side)

2f.

2g.

3 Finish the hem.

3a. Fold the bottom hem of the skirt over ¾" (2 cm) twice. Press. Topstitch using a ¾" (2 cm) seam allowance.

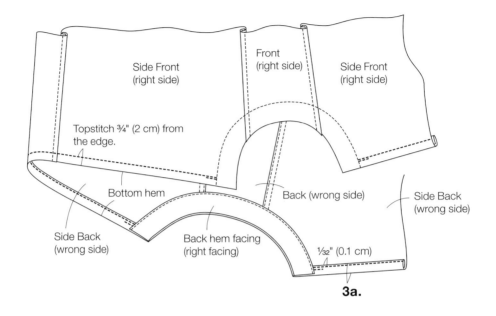

Side Front (right side)

Front (right side)

Side Front (right side)

Topstitch ¾" (2 cm) from the edge.

Bottom hem

Back (wrong side)

Side Back (wrong side)

Side Back (wrong side)

Back hem facing (right facing)

¹⁄₃₂" (0.1 cm)

3a.

4 Finish the waistband.

4a. With right sides together, sew the front waist facings together at center front using ¼" (0.5 cm) long seams to leave an opening for the elastic tape.

4b. Press the center front seam allowance open and stitch both seam allowances down using ¼" (0.5 cm) seam allowances.

4c. With right sides together, sew the front waist facing to the back waist facing. Press the seam allowances open.

4d. Fold the facing hem over ⅜" (1 cm). Press.

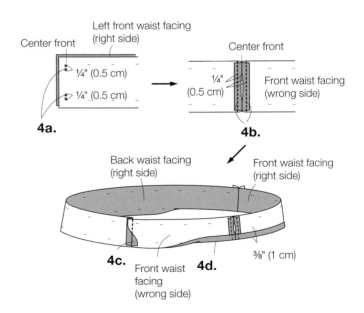

Center front

Left front waist facing (right side)

¼" (0.5 cm)

¼" (0.5 cm)

4a.

Center front

¼" (0.5 cm)

Front waist facing (wrong side)

4b.

Back waist facing (right side)

Front waist facing (right side)

Front waist facing (wrong side)

4c.

⅜" (1 cm)

4d.

4 Finish the waistband (continued).

4e. Align the right side of the waist facing with the wrong side of the skirt.

4f. Sew the waist facing to the skirt using a ⅜" (1 cm) seam allowance.

4g. Fold the waist facing to the right side of the skirt.

4h. On the right side, topstitch the waist facing using three seams.

4i. Insert a ⅜" × 27½" (0.9 × 70 cm) elastic tape through each of the two waistband channels.

4j. Overlap each end of the elastic tape ⅜"–⅝" (1–1.5 cm) and stitch to secure.

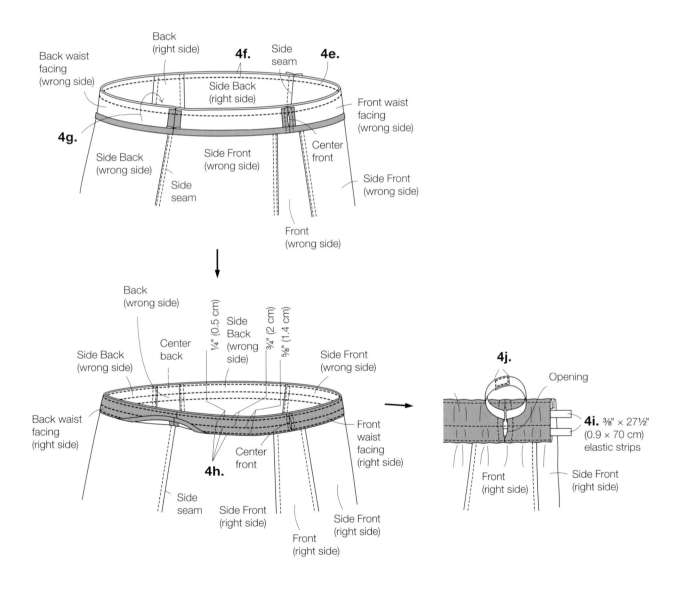

5 Insert the tie.

5a. Fold the long edges over ⅜" (1 cm) each. Press.

5b. Fold the short edges over ⅜" (1 cm) each. Press.

5c. On the right side, fold the tie in half. Press.

5d. Topstitch around the entire tie using a ¹⁄₃₂" (0.1 cm) seam allowance.

5e. Using a bodkin, thread the tie through the waistband.

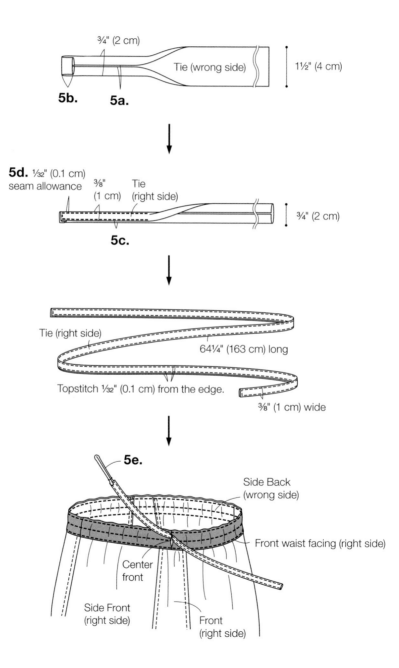

Long Stole/Vest

Page 33 │ This garment combines two different colors of sheer textured fabric to create a wearable work of art. Simply slip it on to wear it as a long stole, fold and fasten it in the back for an origami-like vest, or tie it in front to show off the natural drape. Choose the style that suits you best depending on your outfit and mood!

Materials

Fabric A: Cotton voile
30" × 110" (76 cm × 2.8 m)

Fabric B: Cotton voile
30" × 92¾" (76 cm × 2.35 m)

One ½" (1.3 cm) snap

Small scrap of fabric to cover the snap

Pattern (Side D)

Stole

(Piece for this project is noted as *j* on pattern sheet.)

Cutting Notes

There are no pattern pieces for the bias strips. See cutting diagram on the following page for dimensions.

Cut the pattern from each fabric separately in order to prevent the fabric from slipping.

Note that the armholes are cut out after Fabric A and B have been sewn together.

Sewing Tips

Don't skip the basting steps. It is important to baste the fabrics together before cutting out the armholes in order to hold the fabric in place and ensure that the armholes align.

Cutting Diagram

Fabric A and B

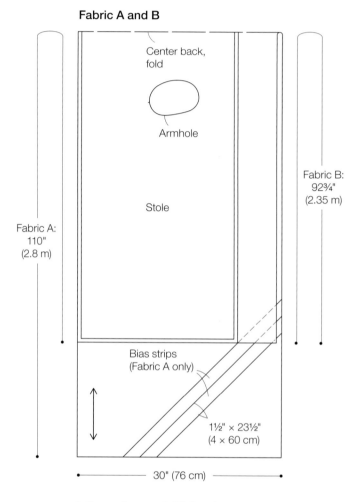

Center back, fold

Armhole

Stole

Fabric B: 92¾" (2.35 m)

Fabric A: 110" (2.8 m)

Bias strips (Fabric A only)

1½" × 23½" (4 × 60 cm)

30" (76 cm)

✱ Seam allowance is ⅜" (1 cm).

Construction Steps Overview

1 Sew Fabric A and B together.

2 Cut out the armholes and turn the stole right side out.

3 Finish the armholes.

4 Cover the snap and attach it to the stole.

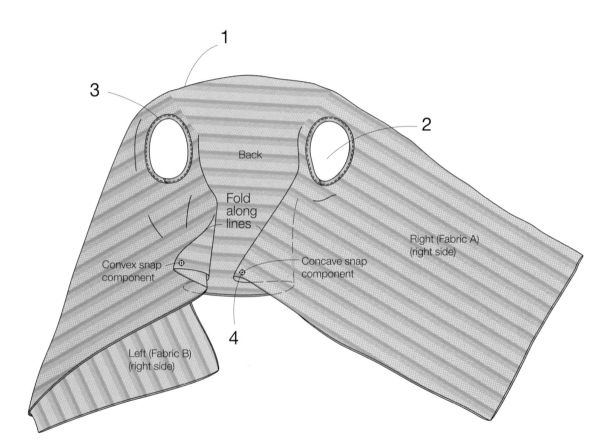

Back

Fold
along
lines

Convex snap
component

Concave snap
component

Right (Fabric A)
(right side)

Left (Fabric B)
(right side)

1 Sew Fabric A and B together.

1a. With right sides together, sew Fabrics A and B using a ⅜" (1 cm) seam allowance. Trim the corner seam allowances.

2 Cut out the armholes and turn the stole right side out.

2a. Mark the armhole seam allowances at ⅜" (1 cm).

2b. Baste around the armholes to hold Fabrics A and B together.

2c. Cut out the armholes.

2d. Remove the basting stitches.

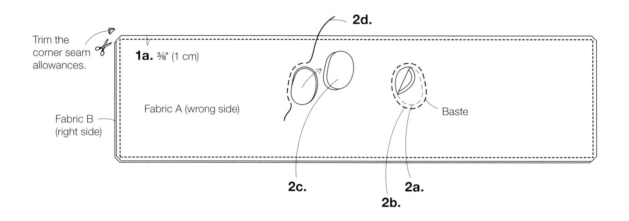

Trim the corner seam allowances.

2d.

1a. ⅜" (1 cm)

Fabric A (wrong side)

Fabric B (right side)

Baste

2c.

2b.

2a.

3 Finish the armholes.

3a. Baste around the armhole using a ¼" (0.5 cm) seam allowance.

3b. Fold one long edge of the bias strip over ⅜" (1 cm). Press.

3c. Fold one short edge of the bias strip over ⅜" (1 cm). Press.

3d. Overlap the short edges of the bias strip.

3e. With right sides together, sew the bias strip to the armhole using a ⅜" (1 cm) seam allowance.

3f. Wrap the bias strip around the seam allowance and topstitch on the right side of the stole using a ⅜" (1 cm) seam allowance. Repeat steps 3a.–3f. for the other armhole.

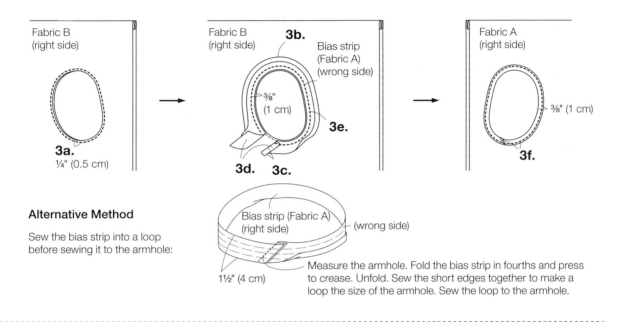

Alternative Method

Sew the bias strip into a loop before sewing it to the armhole:

Measure the armhole. Fold the bias strip in fourths and press to crease. Unfold. Sew the short edges together to make a loop the size of the armhole. Sew the loop to the armhole.

4 Cover the snap and attach it to the stole.

4a. Sew a running stitch around the edge of a circular scrap of fabric.

4b. Use a stiletto to punch a small hole in the center of the fabric.

4c. Cover the convex snap component with the fabric, allowing the snap to protrude through the hole in the fabric. Gather the thread around the base of the snap. Repeat steps 4a.–4c. to cover the concave snap component. Attach the snap components to the stole following the pattern marks.

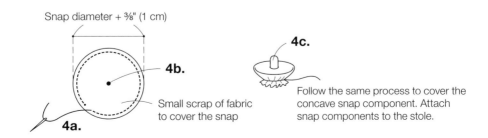

Seamless Wrap Skirt

Page 36 | You can wear this skirt two ways: overlap it in the front for a figure-flattering wrap skirt, or overlap it in the back for a more flared silhouette. Consider using home décor fabric since the seamless design of this skirt suits large patterns. Opt for fabric with nice drape, such as cotton or thin linen.

Materials

Main fabric: Printed cotton/linen
(S): 41¼" × 83" (105 cm × 2.1 m)
(M): 41¼" x 89½" (105 cm x 2.3 m)
(L): 41¼" x 96" (105 cm × 2.5 m)

Accent fabric (for waist facing): Cotton
(S): 15¾" × 39½" (40 cm × 1 m)
(M): 15¾" × 42¾" (40 cm x 1.1 m)
(L): 15¾" x 46" (40 cm x 1.2 m)

Medium-weight fusible interfacing
(for waist facing):
(S): 15¾" × 39½" (40 cm × 1 m)
(M): 15¾" × 42¾" (40 cm × 1.1 m)
(L): 15¾" x 46" (40 cm x 1.2 m)

Fusible bias tape: ⅜" × 94½" (1 cm × 2.4 m)

Pattern (Side D)

Skirt, Waist Facing

(Pieces for this project are noted as *k* on pattern sheet.)

Cutting Notes

The pattern is for half of the skirt. Trace the right side of the pattern, flip it over and join at the fold line, then continue tracing the wrong side of the pattern to make the whole skirt pattern.

Note that length of the skirt differs on the right and left sides.

There are no pattern pieces for the ties, belt loops, or opening facing. See the diagrams on the following page for dimensions.

Sewing Tips

It is important to press the hem seam allowances carefully in order to achieve neatly finished corners.

Before You Begin Sewing

Affix fusible bias tape to both short edges of the skirt.

Cutting Diagrams

Main Fabric

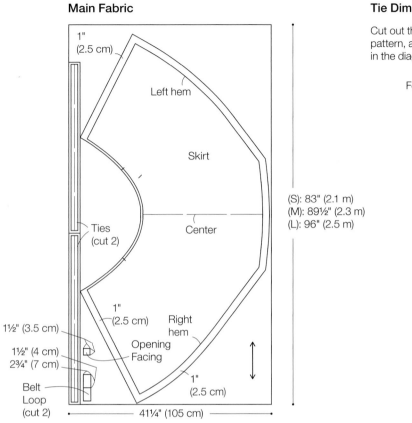

1"
(2.5 cm)

Left hem

Skirt

Center

Ties
(cut 2)

1"
(2.5 cm)

Right
hem

Opening
Facing

1"
(2.5 cm)

1½" (3.5 cm)

1½" (4 cm)
2¾" (7 cm)

Belt
Loop
(cut 2)

(S): 83" (2.1 m)
(M): 89½" (2.3 m)
(L): 96" (2.5 m)

41¼" (105 cm)

✳ Seam allowance is ⅜" (1 cm), unless otherwise noted.

Tie Dimensions

Cut out the ties, which have no pattern, according to the dimensions in the diagram below.

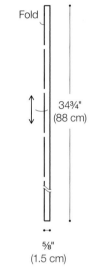

Fold

34¾"
(88 cm)

⅝"
(1.5 cm)

Accent Fabric

Center front,
Fold

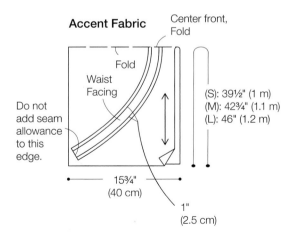

Fold

Waist
Facing

Do not
add seam
allowance
to this
edge.

(S): 39½" (1 m)
(M): 42¾" (1.1 m)
(L): 46" (1.2 m)

15¾"
(40 cm)

1"
(2.5 cm)

Construction Steps Overview

1 Make the ties.

2 Make an opening for the tie.

3 Finish the waist facing.

4 Finish the corners.

5 Finish the sides and attach the ties.

6 Finish the hem.

7 Attach the belt loops.

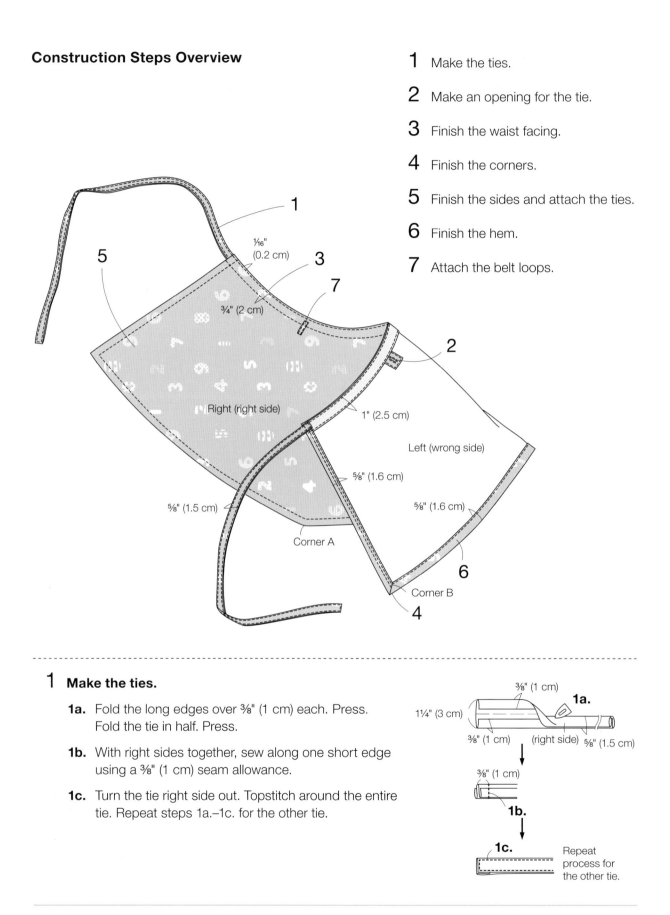

1

5

3

7

¹⁄₁₆" (0.2 cm)

¾" (2 cm)

2

Right (right side)

1" (2.5 cm)

Left (wrong side)

⅝" (1.6 cm)

⅝" (1.5 cm)

⅝" (1.6 cm)

Corner A

Corner B

6

4

---

1 Make the ties.

1a. Fold the long edges over ⅜" (1 cm) each. Press. Fold the tie in half. Press.

1b. With right sides together, sew along one short edge using a ⅜" (1 cm) seam allowance.

1c. Turn the tie right side out. Topstitch around the entire tie. Repeat steps 1a.–1c. for the other tie.

⅜" (1 cm)

1a.

1¼" (3 cm)

⅜" (1 cm)

(right side)   ⅝" (1.5 cm)

⅜" (1 cm)

1b.

1c.

Repeat process for the other tie.

2 Make an opening for the tie.

2a. Fold ¼" (0.5 cm) seam allowances along the sides and bottom of the opening facing. Press to crease. On the left side of the skirt, align the opening facing and skirt with right sides together. Sew the opening facing to the skirt following the pattern mark and using small stitches.

2b. Carefully cut a slit through both the opening facing and the skirt. Pull the facing through the slit to the wrong side of the skirt. Press.

2c. On the wrong side of the skirt, topstitch around the opening.

2d. Topstitch around the sides and bottom of the opening facing to secure.

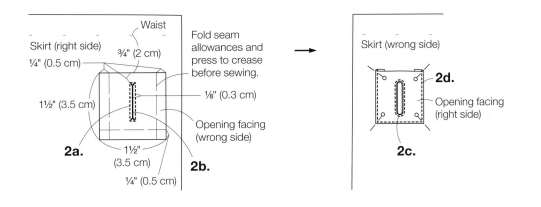

3 Finish the waist facing.

3a. Fuse interfacing and affix fusible bias tape to the wrong side of the waist facing. Fold the seam allowance and press.

3b. Align the waist facing and skirt with right sides together, making sure to position the waist facing 1" (2.5 cm) from the edge of the skirt. Sew the waist facing to the skirt using a ⅜" (1 cm) seam allowance.

3c. Fold the waist facing to the wrong side of the skirt. Press. Topstitch the waist facing with two seams about ¾" (2 cm) apart.

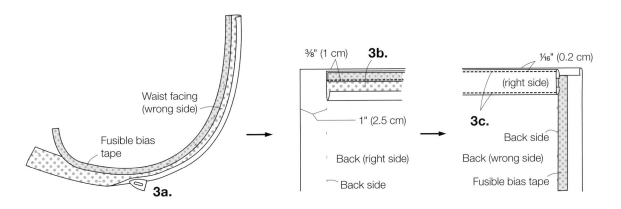

4 Finish the corners.

Corner A

4a. Fold ⅝" (1.6 cm) to the right side. Press, then fold ⅜" (0.9 cm) back and press. Fold the corner seam allowance and stitch, sewing through the two seam allowance layers only, as if making a dart.

4b. Fold the seam allowance to the wrong side and press to prepare for topstitching the hem.

Corner B

4c. Fold the side of the skirt over ⅜" (0.9 cm). Press. Stitch close to the edge.

4d. Fold the bottom of the skirt over ½" (1.2 cm). Press.

4e. Fold the skirt with right sides together and align the • marks. Fold all layers at the seam allowance. Press.

4f. Draw a line across the corner point.

4g. Sew across the corner point using a ¼" (0.5 cm) seam allowance. Trim the excess fabric. Fold the hem at the seam allowance and turn the skirt right side out. Repeat steps 4c.–4g. for the other Corner B.

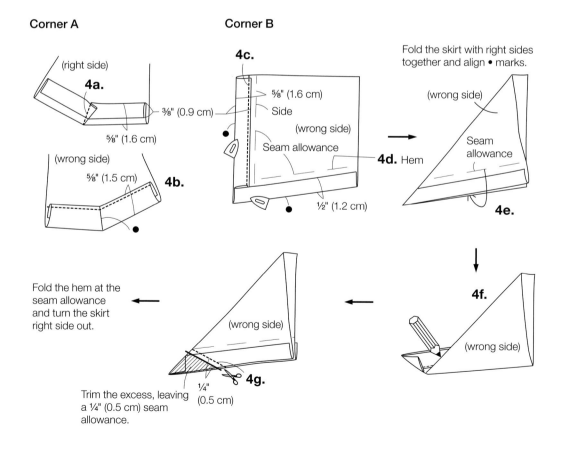

Corner A

Corner B

(right side)

4a.

⅜" (0.9 cm)

⅝" (1.6 cm)

(wrong side)

⅝" (1.5 cm)

4b.

4c.

⅝" (1.6 cm)

Side

(wrong side)

Seam allowance

4d. Hem

½" (1.2 cm)

Fold the skirt with right sides together and align • marks.

(wrong side)

Seam allowance

4e.

4f.

(wrong side)

Fold the hem at the seam allowance and turn the skirt right side out.

(wrong side)

Trim the excess, leaving a ¼" (0.5 cm) seam allowance.

¼" (0.5 cm)

4g.

5 Finish the sides and attach the ties.

5a. On the wrong side of the skirt, align a tie on top of the waist facing. Baste to secure the tie.

5b. Fold the side of the skirt over ⅝" (1.6 cm) at the seam allowance and sew close to the edge.

5c. Fold the tie over to the wrong side and topstitch to secure. Repeat steps 5a.–5c. for the other side of the skirt.

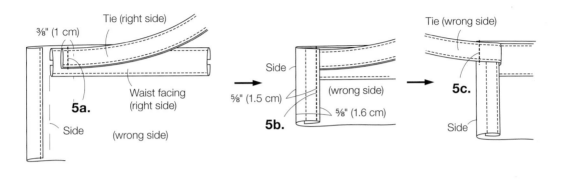

6 Finish the hem.

6a. Topstitch the bottom hem using a ⅝" (1.5 cm) seam allowance.

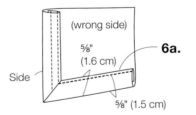

7 Attach the belt loops.

7a. Fold a belt loop in four, following the same method used to fold the ties. Press. Topstitch with two seams about ⅜" (1 cm) apart.

7b. Align the belt loop on the skirt following the pattern mark. Sew across the short end using a ¼" (0.5 cm) seam allowance.

7c. Fold the belt loop up and stitch ⅜" (1 cm) from the edge.

7d. Fold the belt loop down and repeat process to attach the bottom. Repeat steps 7a.–7d. for the other belt loop.

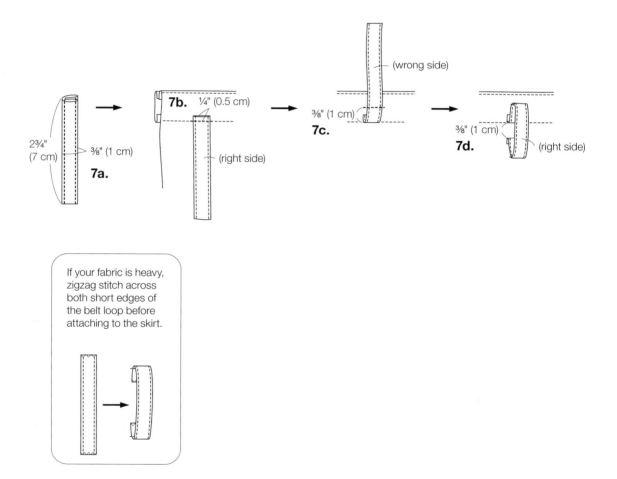

If your fabric is heavy, zigzag stitch across both short edges of the belt loop before attaching to the skirt.

Statement-Making Spiral Brooch

Page 38 | Create this artistic brooch with just a few scraps and some simple hand stitches. Layer sheer fabrics in coordinating shades for some dimension, then arrange the fabric layers to add volume and increase the drama. Whether you pin it to the lapel of your favorite jacket or wear it at the neckline of an old t-shirt, this statement-making accessory will transform your outfit.

Materials

Fabric A: Dark fabric (for A1 and A2)
6" × 11" (15 × 28 cm)

Fabric B: Light fabric (for B1 and B2)
6" × 11" (15 × 28 cm)

One 1¼" (3 cm) safety pin

Pattern (Side D)

Choker/Brooch (Pieces for this project are noted as / on pattern sheet.)

Cutting Notes

Note that each pattern piece has a different circumference.

Sewing Tips

For a neater finished appearance, try to make the handstitching invisible.

Cutting Diagram

Fabric A

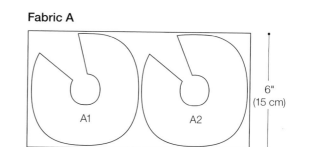

A1   A2

6"
(15 cm)

11" (28 cm)

Fabric B

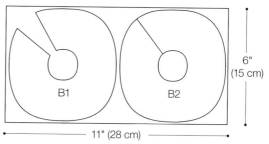

B1   B2

6"
(15 cm)

11" (28 cm)

Construction Steps Overview

1 Align the edges of A1, A2, and B1. Place these three pieces on top of the wrong side of B2. Fold the hem of B2 over twice and blind stitch through four pieces of fabric.

2 Whipstitch the safety pin to the brooch. Try to make the stitches invisible.

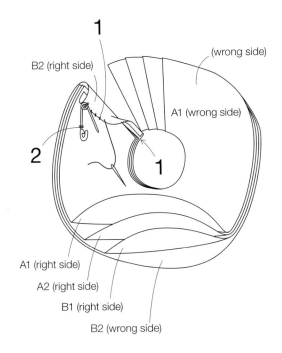

* Adjust the layers of fabric to add dimension to the brooch.

Basic Techniques

How to Sew Snaps

Snap placement

Knot

1. Insert a knotted strand of thread through the right side of the fabric at the snap placement.

Thread loop

2. Insert needle through a snap opening and make a thread loop, then bring the needle through the thread loop.

Buttonhole stitch

3. Pull the thread to secure. Repeat this process, known as the buttonhole stitch, a few times, making sure to stitch through the fabric each time.

Snap opening

4. Bring the needle to the next snap opening.

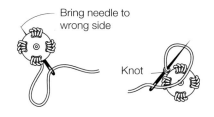

Bring needle to wrong side

Knot

5. Once all the snap openings have been stitched, bring the needle through the fabric to the wrong side. Make a knot.

Knot

6. Bring the needle back to the right side of the fabric. Cut the extra thread very short so the end is hidden behind the snap.

How to Sew Buttons

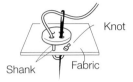

Knot

Shank

Fabric

¼" (0.5 cm) shank

1. Insert a knotted strand of thread through to the wrong side of the fabric. Bring needle back to the right side, through the holes in the button, then back to the wrong side. Leave enough slack in the thread between the button and the fabric in order to form a shank.

2. Stitch through each pair of holes twice.

Shank

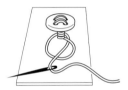

3. Wind the thread around the slack to form a shank. Pull up on the button with one hand and wind thread tightly down toward fabric. The shank will shorten to about ⅛" (0.3 cm) after the thread has been wound.

4. Insert the needle and thread through the last loop.

5. Bring the needle and thread through the fabric to the wrong side.

6. Make a knot and bring the needle back to the right side of the fabric. Cut the extra thread very short so the end is hidden behind the button.

How to Sew Buttonholes

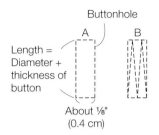

Buttonhole

A   B

Length = Diameter + thickness of button

About ⅛" (0.4 cm)

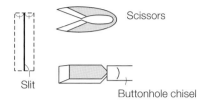

Scissors

Slit

Buttonhole chisel

1. Machine stitch on fabric to mark the buttonhole according to diagram A. If using fabric that frays easily, mark the buttonhole according to diagram B.

2. Cut a vertical slit down the middle of the buttonhole. Use scissors or a buttonhole chisel to cut the slit.

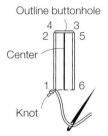

Outline buttonhole

4 3
2 5

Center

1 6

Knot

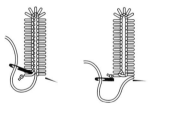

7
8
9
10

Hold completed stitches

3. Insert a knotted strand of thread through the right side of the fabric. Stitch around the outline of the buttonhole following the numerical order shown in the above diagram.

4. Make a thread loop, then bring the needle through the thread loop following the numerical order shown in the above diagram. Pull thread up at a 45° angle and tighten. Hold completed stitches out of the way with a finger as you work.

4–5 stitches

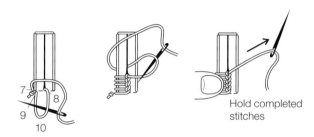

5. For the corner, make four or five stitches, pulling the thread up at a 90-degree angle and tightening.

6. For the end, insert the needle back through the fabric at the first stitch. Make two long horizontal stitches, then two vertical stitches.

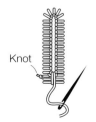

Knot

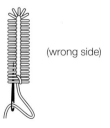

(wrong side)

7. Trim excess thread and hide knot under stitches.

8. Bring the needle to the wrong side of the fabric. Pull the needle and thread underneath a few stitches on the wrong side to secure. Cut the extra thread.

How to Attach Bias Tape

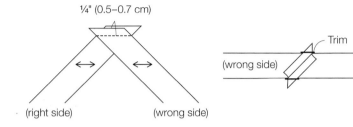

¼" (0.5–0.7 cm)

(right side)   (wrong side)

1. With right sides together, sew bias strips together along short ends using a ¼" (0.5–0.7 cm) seam allowance. Trim the excess.

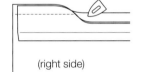

Trim

(wrong side)

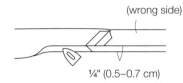

(wrong side)

¼" (0.5–0.7 cm)

2. Fold one long edge over ¼" (0.5–0.7 cm). Press.

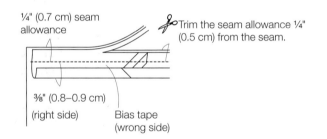

¼" (0.7 cm) seam allowance

Trim the seam allowance ¼" (0.5 cm) from the seam.

⅜" (0.8–0.9 cm)

(right side)   Bias tape (wrong side)

3. With right sides together, sew ¼" (0.7 cm) from the edge. Trim the seam allowance.

(right side)

4. Fold along the stitching and press.

5. Make clips along the curved section of the seam allowance. Fold the seam allowance along the stitching and press.

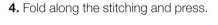

¼" (0.7 cm)

(right side)

6. Topstitch on right side.

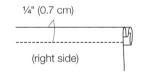

Glossary

Running stitch: the basic hand sewing stitch made by passing the needle in and out of the fabric.

Invisible zipper: a type of zipper that looks like a seam when closed. Use an invisible zipper if you don't want the opening to be easily noticeable.

Basting: long, easily removable stitching used to temporarily hold pieces of fabric together or to mark a fold line.

Reinforcement stitching: short machine stitches (12–14 stitches per inch) used to strengthen areas that receive a lot of wear, such as corners.

Right sides together: align the fabric so the sides you want visible on the finished garment are facing each other.

Press the seam allowance open: after sewing two pieces of fabric together, open and press so the seam allowance lies flat.

Bias strip: a strip of fabric cut out at a 45-degree angle to the warp of the fabric grain. Bias strips are often used to finish curved seam allowances, such as armholes and hems.

Facing: a piece of fabric that finishes an opening, such as a neckline, armhole, or waistline, so that the wrong side of the fabric and seams are not visible on the finished garment.

Topstitch: stitching on the right side of the fabric used to reinforce seams or for decorative effect.

Selvage: the raw edge of the fabric where the weft threads of the fabric grain change direction. The selvage is occasionally incorporated into a garment's design because it does not fray.

Fusible interfacing: a type of interfacing with an adhesive material on one side that is activated with heat from the iron. Interfacing adds structure to fabric and helps garments keep their shape. The designs in this book often call for lightweight or medium-weight interfacing.

Fusible tape: a thin strip of fusible interfacing used to stabilize the fabric and prevent stretching. The designs in this book use two varieties of fusible tape: regular and bias. The regular fusible tape is used on straight edges, such as along the center front edges of a bodice. Fusible bias tape is used on areas that stretch easily, such as along curves. necklines and armholes. The tape is usually ¼"–¾" (0.5–2 cm) in width.

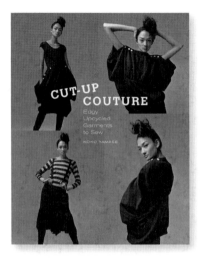